COLLECTIBLE CLOTHING

with prices

Sheila Malouff

Cover design by Heather Miller
Cover etching from *Victorian Fashions and Costumes
from Harper's Bazar*, 1867-1898; ©Stella Blum, Dover Publications,
New York

Photographs (unless otherwise credited) by Gary Meyer,
Meyer Photography, Pueblo, Colorado

Library of Congress
Catalog Number 82-061785

ISBN 0-87069-423-5

Published by

Wallace-Homestead Book Company
1912 Grand Avenue
Des Moines, Iowa 50305

This book is dedicated to my husband Charles, my daughter Rochelle, and my son Andrew, for their patience and encouragement. I also dedicate this book to all people, with the hope that the dream of world peace may soon be a reality.

Acknowledgments

This book would not have been possible without the cooperation and assistance of many individuals. I would like to extend a special thank-you to the following for graciously loaning garments from their private collections or inventories to be photographed for this book: Loretta Fortier of Montage in Houston, Texas; Second Hand Rose in New Orleans, Louisiana; Pearl of The Flamingo Gallery in Colorado Springs, Colorado; Puttin' on the Ritz in Atlanta, Georgia; and Pamela's Reminiscence in St. Augustine, Florida.

I would also like to thank my photographer, Gary Meyer of Meyer Photography, Pueblo, Colorado, for his patience and creativity and Stella Blum and Dover Publications, N.Y., for their gracious permission to reproduce illustrations from *Victorian Fashions and Costumes from Harper's Bazar, 1867-1898*. A special thanks goes to my husband, Charles, for his legal expertise. Thanks also to my mother and father who taught me the real meaning of the word *live*, and to Ange and Frank Pantleo, for caring for my children as they would their own. Thanks to all of my relatives and friends for their encouragement and prayers.

Contents

Introduction

A wonderful new field of collecting has blossomed in the United States in recent years. Vintage clothing collecting is rapidly becoming a widely recognized field in the world of antiques and collectibles.

Collecting vintage clothing is exciting because one rarely finds two identical pieces. The collectible clothing field is unlike collecting depression glass, for example, which has standard styles and pieces, and therefore can be described and priced easily.

Unless you have a vivid imagination, it is nearly impossible to see what a garment actually looks like from a written description. Therefore, to help you price clothing effectively numerous photographs have been provided in this book. It literally would be impossible to provide a photograph for every piece of clothing that is collectible, but an attempt has been made to provide the widest variety of items possible.

This book should be considered only as a guide to vintage clothing prices. Prices in this book reflect an average of retail prices at numerous vintage clothing stores around the country. Retail prices vary from city to city, state to state, of course, with the highest prices seen in larger metropolitan areas, such as New York City, or the Los Angeles area. Prices naturally are higher in high-rent districts, as dealers must create a larger profit to meet their overhead.

Keep in mind that many variables contribute to a garment's price. The garments and accessories priced in this book are in excellent to mint condition, except where noted. Designer labels, sizes, fabrics, trims and many other details influence the price of a garment, too. Therefore, just because one item looks like another does not mean that the prices for the two will be the same. One garment may be a designer original, while the other may not be, which would make the original worth much more.

Common sense is called for when using a price guide to purchase a vintage garment for your wardrobe or collection. The ultimate decision concerning the price to pay must be yours. Garments are ultimately worth whatever the buyer is willing to pay. If you like something, and you feel the price is fair, then buy it and enjoy.

Prices for the garments in the photographs loaned by Sotheby Parke-Bernet are not prices achieved at auction. The prices listed in this book were set by the author.

Collecting vintage clothing can be fun and profitable. It can also be addictive—so beware!

Neither the author nor the publisher assumes responsibility for any losses that might occur as a result of using this guide to purchase or sell vintage clothing. Prices are given to serve merely as a guide.

The History of Fashion

Ladies' Fashions

Clothing has existed for centuries, mostly as a means of covering and protecting the body. But as early as the ancient Egyptians, fashion in dress can be observed. Fashion has always been an indicator of social status. As early Egyptian history shows, servants and peasants wore plain short skirts or loincloths, while the upper class had fancier versions of the same. Fashions in the early days changed rapidly, just as fashions do today.

Until the nineteenth century, clothing was mostly handmade. But with the invention of the sewing machine in the 1800s, a dramatic change occurred. Fashion became industrialized. Along with industrialization came a new phenomenon called *designers*, and Paris, where many of the designers were located, became a major fashion center.

The man who was largely responsible for the fashion industry in Paris in the 1800s was Charles Frederic Worth. The fashion house of Worth began in the 1870s and continued in his family until 1956. Clothing made by Worth was an expensive luxury only the wealthy could afford. Garments or accessories with the Worth label are avidly sought today and bring high prices, as do other designer originals.

As Worth was preparing for his career in designing during the 1860s, fashion itself was changing rapidly. As women were becoming more active, fashions were changing to meet their need for freer movement.

Before the 1870s, dresses were always worn with large bustles in the back and hoops. Dresses were made of rich silks, trimmed with ribbons and fine quality laces.

Accessories were as important as the dress itself. Small hats with tiny plumes and flowers sat smartly on hair that was uniquely braided or finger waved.

But during the 1870s, fashion took on a more natural look. Bustles were narrowed somewhat, and there were changes in the trimmings of the dresses. The silk flowers and lavish ribbon trimmings of the 1860s were replaced by heavier braid passementerie and fringes. Hats became a little smaller, coiffures became fancier, and lavish hair ornaments, made of tortoise or guttapercha, became popular.

Lingerie was an important part of one's wardrobe, too. Most lingerie was made of cotton or linen ornately embroidered or lavishly trimmed with laces, eyelets and tucks. All garments were white, and silks were used only occasionally for corsets and petticoats.

As women became more active in sports during the 1880s, fashion followed with more practical concepts. Sportswear, such as riding and hunting suits, were seen more often. Bustles remained popular, even for sportswear, but the heavy trains disappeared to make for easier walking. Fabrics as well as trims were heavier. Hats were still small, but were lavishly decorated. Along with the ordinary types of laces and hat trims, an unusual decorative item was added during this time—birds. Yes, birds! These hats with bird trimmings were to remain popular until around 1898 when suddenly they were no longer seen. These hats are highly collectible today.

Dresses by Worth, Pacquin, Doucet, Callot Soeurs, Redfern and other famous designers appealed to wealthy Americans during the 1890s. Wealthy ladies who were fortunate to travel abroad would come back to America from Paris with luxurious designer dresses and accessories. Exquisite silks and satins were used profusely in the making of these garments, which were lavishly trimmed with beaded passementeries or were richly hand-embroidered. Those less fortunate would purchase patterns and try to make their own renditions of the popular styles. Although the quality of the homemade items did not match those of the original designer dresses, the fabrics that were used, and the fact that they were handmade, makes them collectible garments today.

During the 1890s, sportswear became increasingly popular as women became more and more active. Golfing and bicycling were the most popular sports for women. Many bicycling costumes — knickers, bloomers or skirts—were made of alpaca, serge or lightweight cotton. Jackets were made of white pique or linen. Small sailor hats, black silk stockings, and black leather pointed shoes completed the outfit for a day of cycling.

Fashion at this time was also influenced by the popularity of the Gibson Girl in America. Women dressed in similar-looking shirtwaists and skirts, and even styled their hair in an upsweep, with a delicately trimmed hat perched precariously on top to complete the American look. Waists were still tightly corseted, and skirts became more narrow over the hips and at the hemline. Bustles were still worn, but beginning to disappear. Bodices were high-necked with huge balloon sleeves, as seen on posters by the famous artist Toulouse-Lautrec.

With the turn of the century and the advent of the Edwardian period came the "new woman," a woman concerned with her rights. Fashions changed, too, as tailor-made suits with plain tailored shirts were suddenly seen. The less frilly, feminine look suited the "business woman," although there were few of them.

But femininity was still apparent in the lavish dresses and gowns boasting laces, ribbons, beadwork and exquisitie embroideries. Most dresses were made of lovely fabrics including chiffons, soft faille, crepe de chine, and cashmere. These dresses had a small-waisted look, which means most ladies were still wearing tightly laced corsets.

Volume XV.   Number 9, 1895.

September

TOILETTES

NEW AND ORIGINAL BICYCLE COSTUME.

Price,
20 Cents.

Toilettes Publishing Company,
126 WEST TWENTY-THIRD STREET, NEW YORK.

$1.50
A Year.

Lingerie was lacier than ever. Crisp white cotton undergarments, trimmed with lavish eyelets were standard. Hats were still worn for every occasion, were wide-brimmed and heavily trimmed with silk flowers and plumes. Accessories included ostrich and marabou boas, fur muffs and stoles, elaborate capes, and lacy parasols.

At the same time, bicycling and other sports activities were more popular than ever. Bloomers and knickers were pared down to allow for easier movement.

Paris was still the center of fashion, and wealthy women were still avidly seeking the fashions designed by Callot Soeurs and Worth. Paul Poiret made his appearance on the fashion scene around 1910. He was the one who changed the course of fashion drastically by introducing a "natural" look, denouncing the corset. The full-busted, small waist and bustle look was beginning to disappear. Women could breathe once again.

Many of the lacy frills of past decades began to disappear, too. Bodices were high-waisted, and high necklines were replaced with lower, rounded necklines. V-necklines were starting to appear. Tailored suits with loose-waisted jackets and straight ankle-length walking skirts with solid lines and pleats became commonplace.

Around 1910, a young woman by the name of Gabrielle Chanel opened her first millinery shop in Deauville, France. This was the beginning of a successful lifelong career that would make Chanel one of the most famous designers of this century. Another designer, Mariano Fortuny of Venice, started producing his lavish capes and dresses, which were avidly sought by the wealthy. A master of fabric design, his career, too, was just beginning.

The first fashion show of American designs was held in 1914. New York City hosted the show, which was presented by Mrs. Edna Woolman Chase, editor of *Vogue* magazine. The designers included Herman Patrick Tappe, Henri Bendel and Bergdorf Goodman. This marked the beginning of a growing reputation for New York City as a fashion capital.

With the advent of World War I, fashion in the United States suddenly took on a more practical, less dramatic look. Clothes were designed with the working woman in mind. After the war ended, drastic changes in fashion transpired. For the first few years fashion was erratic. Hemlines were up and down. Fashion didn't seem to have any direction. But eventually out of the confusion came a rather unusual look, unusual compared with previous decades, that is. Shapeless, boyish clothes became popular, as well as boyish-style hairdos. Cloche hats, which fit the head tightly, were occasionally decorated with feathers, beadwork, or celluloid buckles. Dresses were loose and straight. Waistlines could no longer be seen. Chiffon, georgette, crepe de chine, satin and lace were popular fabrics. Lavish embroidery and heavy beadwork adorned the flapper-period evening dresses.

The effect of Art Deco, a geometric style that came out of the Paris Exposition of 1925, could be seen in the clothing, hats, combs, purses, compacts and other accessories of the American woman. Long cigarette holders were a must for the chic look.

Gabrielle "CoCo" Chanel had gained recognition as an international designer by the mid-1920s. Most of her designs were casual, yet elegant, and are classics today.

One of the most glorious designers of our century, Mariano Fortuny, blessed the 1920s with his graceful, flowing, pleated dresses. These dresses, available in assorted rich colors, were pleated by a special process that he alone created. Only the very wealthy knew of his fabulous designs, which were adorned with lavish Venetian glass beads. The dresses, when purchased, were rolled and tucked neatly into a small hatbox to keep the pleats intact. Dresses had to be returned to Venice for cleaning and repleating. These dresses are rare and highly collectible today, with prices ranging from $1,500 up.

At this time, too, Elsa Schiaparelli, an Italian, was quickly establishing herself as a leading fashion designer. She eventually opened a fashion studio in the Place Vendome in Paris. In the late 1920s she changed the course of fashion history by rejecting the cloche as a suitable hat. She also introduced colors that would eventually change the fashion industry. She carried her career successfully through the 1930s.

Another designer in the 1900s who drastically changed the course of fashion history was Jean Patou. His styles took on a completely different look. Around 1929 he lowered hemlines and brought the waistline back to a normal position. He also began manufacturing perfumes. Joy, his most famous scent, was the world's most expensive perfume for years. Other important designers of the 1920s included Captain Edward Molyneux, Lucien Le Long, Madeleine Vionnet, Hattie Carnegie, Jessie Franklin Turner, Nettie Rosenstein, Vincent Monte-Sano, Philip Mangone, Anthony Blotta, Helen Cookman, Clare Potter, and Sydney Wragge.

The Wall Street Crash of 1929 brought about drastic changes in the fashion world. Paris was suddenly no longer the fashion capital. Skirts grew longer and a more feminine shape reappeared. Glamour was the fashion trend of the 1930s with emphasis on the motion picture industry. Adrian, the designer of the stars, was popular at this time. His clients included Greta Garbo.

Jean Harlow made the bias-cut evening dress popular. Stores across America were filled with copies of dresses worn by her and other famous movie stars of the day. The Harlow-style evening dresses were tight fitting and sleeveless, with low scooped backlines and bias cut for a gentle flared hemline.

Beautiful feminine lingerie made of silks or rayons, usually peach or pastel blue in color and trimmed with ecru laces, was popular. The most revealing swimwear ever, appeared. Accessories included fur boas and hats, which were found in a variety of shapes and sizes.

Cristobal Balenciaga, a Spanish-born designer, opened his first fashion house in the early 1930s in San Sebastian. Successful with this first fashion house, he later opened a second house in Madrid and a third in Paris in 1937. His designs were classical, yet sculptured.

Other important designers of the 1930s were Captain Edward Molyneux, Mainbocher, Chanel, Vionnet, Le Long, Jean Patou, Creed, Valentina, Charles James, Hattie Carnegie, Leslie Morris of Bergdorf Goodman, Sophie of Saks Fifth Avenue, Nettie Rosenstein, Omar Kiam, Ben Reig, Dorothy Shaver of Lord and Taylor, Claire McCardell, Clare Potter, Bonnie Cashin, Vera Maxwell, Tina Leser, and Sydney Wragge. Watch for their labels.

Heightening of the shoulders appeared in the late 1930s and lasted throughout the 1940s. Floral-printed rayon and silks were popular for day and evening wear in the pre-World War II era. With the onset of World War II, fashions took the backstage. Styles and fabrics were very conservative. Dresses used as little fabric as possible. Suits with classic lines and high padded shoulders were popular. The quality of most of these garments is difficult to find in clothing made today. Most were made of durable fabrics such as gabardine or tweed and were lined with satin or rayon crepe. The classic style of the 1940s is still fashionable today.

In the postwar period, more colorful and fashionable styles were seen in magazines and on a new and important invention — television. It was around this time that Christian Dior, a French designer, changed the course of fashion history with his "new look." Rounded shoulders, full skirts and tiny waistlines dominated the fashion scene. Also instrumental with the success of the new look was Pierre Balmain, a French-born fashion designer who worked closely with Dior. Other inspiring designers of this period included Lucien Le Long and Cristobal Balenciaga.

The new look remained stylish throughout the first half of the 1950s. In 1955 Christian Dior again made fashion news with the creation of the A-line. During the 1950s synthethic fabrics were invented and used more frequently. Stiff net and lace adorned these fabrics. Gone were the outrageous floral prints and peplums, which were replaced by plaids and solids and straight lines.

Bobby socks with saddle oxfords and circle skirts with starched blouses in solid colors were the style of the music era called "rock and roll." The beaded sweaters and full-net prom dresses of the 1950s are sought today as 1950s parties and "sock hops" abound.

Fashions for Men

Fashions for men have always changed at a slower pace than they do for women. In fact, the basic design of the suit has not changed much since the turn of the century. From the late 1800s to about 1910, knee-length frock coats were the common style. But in 1910 the natural shoulder suit made its entrance. The single-breasted jacket had narrow lapels, and the trousers were straight.

From 1890 to about 1916, shirts with high, stiff collars and starched bib fronts were popular. Most of the attachable collars were made of celluloid. After the early 1900s, shirts with soft, attached collars became the style. These shirts are still stylish today. Palm beach cloth, a light porous fabric, was patented in 1907 and used as a fabric in men's clothing. Seersucker, also produced about this time, was a popular fabric for summer suits.

Beige was the popular color in the 1920s, and men's clothing no longer seemed quite as formal, both in style and color. Double-breasted "zoot" suits with cuffed, wide-legged trousers were introduced. The sports shirt of the late 1920s, called the gaucho, could be found in fabrics of silk, cotton, flannel and rayon. Plaid shirts were also becoming popular.

Suede and leather jackets surfaced in California in the early 1940s, especially the flight jacket style, which resembled the jacket worn by bombardiers. Navy pea jackets were also popular. The suburban coat, a cross between a topcoat and a sports jacket, appeared in the 1950s.

Since the 1920s, clothing for men has become increasingly casual-looking. The casual look was especially popular with California designers and manufacturers in the early 1940s. It was the California designers who first created the western look. Western-style clothes have always been popular, and these vintage garments are especially collectible today. Gabardine shirts with pearl snaps and lavish embroidery always bring healthy prices at specialty shops. Tropical prints were everywhere during the 1940s and 1950s. Rayon Hawaiian-labeled shirts were in vogue then and are still collectible for wear today.

Hats have always been an essential part of every well-dressed man's wardrobe. They were often made of expensive fabrics and trims, such as beaver skin and silk. Top hats, derbies and straw boaters were popular until the 1930s, when fedoras came into fashion. Hats began to lose their popularity in the 1950s and are only rarely worn today.

Bow ties and four-in-hand neckties, popular around 1890, remained in style until the 1930s when contemporary style shirts became popular. It was in the 1930s that the contemporary knotted tie came into existence. Heavy silk was the traditional fabric for men's ties, and patterns changed very little. Stripes, paisley prints, and polka dots have always been popular. Hand-painted ties were in demand in the 1940s and are quite collectible today. Ties became narrow in the 1950s, and those made of iridescent silk fabrics are still stylish.

Children's Fashions

During the late 1800s, children's clothes were as elaborate as the dresses their mothers wore. Little girls were dressed in frilly garments adorned with much lace. Little boys wore sailor suits made of lavish fabrics such as velvet. It was also fashionable for a short while for boys to wear dresses.

Beautiful white cotton, long christening dresses for infants were popular, too, in the

1800s. They were lavishly trimmed with laces or delicately embroidered. Petticoats of cotton and lace were worn beneath them. The gowns occasionally exceeded forty-five inches in length. Tiny white kid-leather high-button shoes and hand-crocheted, lace-trimmed bonnets with silk ribbons completed the outfits.

By the turn of the century, a gradual change could be seen. Little girls' dresses were becoming more practical for daytime apparel. The frilly dresses were saved for special occasions. Knickers became popular wearing apparel for boys, but sailor suits were still being worn.

Children's fashions changed drastically in the early 1920s. Little girls' clothes took on a boyish look just as their mothers' clothes did. Boys' clothing became more masculine looking. Long christening gowns were still popular, but not quite as elaborate.

After the 1920s, children's clothing became much the same as it is today. Collecting children's clothing is unlike collecting ladies' or men's clothing in the respect that only the earliest pieces, and some made in the 1920s, are collectible and have value.

Collecting Vintage Clothing

How to Buy Collectible Clothing

Clothing, like any other collectible, is less valuable if it is damaged. Condition is one of the most important aspects to consider when deciding whether to buy a piece for your collection or wardrobe. Garments in mint condition (that means *no* stains, holes or noticeable repairs) are the best buys. Hold a garment up to a bright light to check for moth or cigarette holes.

If you come across a beautiful vintage garment with some damage, you should consider the following before you decide to buy it: Is the damage easily repairable? If a garment simply needs buttons, or a small seam sewn, then it really should not be considered seriously damaged, although a discount should be given. However, if there are tears in the fabric or moth holes (which are difficult to repair without reweaving, which is expensive), then the garment is greatly devalued and should not be purchased unless you can use the trimming, lace, or some other part to repair another garment.

If a garment is yellowed or stained, it should be purchased only if it is made of a durable fabric, such as cotton or linen. Most yellowing and stains will come out of garments made of these fabrics if washed properly. Silks, wools and synthetics are a different story. Stains that have been in these fabrics for years rarely can be removed. Underarm stains are the worst and should be avoided completely. Garments with fading under the arms or elsewhere should also be avoided. Do not let others convince you that the garment can be dyed to hide stains. Faded spots will usually show up even on a dyed garment. Garments that simply need a good dry cleaning to eliminate dust collected over the years should be discounted to allow for professional cleaning.

Linen and cottons are your best bets for Victorian and Edwardian pieces, as they are more durable fabrics. Be careful of silks from these periods, as silk deteriorates over time, especially if a garment is not stored properly. Presently, the best investment in clothing is Victorian and Edwardian cotton and linen garments, including dresses, blouses, and undergarments. Petticoats currently are being worn for skirts, with camisoles worn as blouses. Black Victorian clothes are generally not as collectible, and are worth less. Handmade clothing and clothing with hand-embroidery, handmade lace, beadwork or lavish trims are always good investments.

Watch for designer labels, which are of the greatest value in vintage clothes. Most designer-label garments were hand-tailored and are one of a kind. They are highly collectible today, and bring high prices at many of the major auction houses across the country. Labels were not always sewn into the collar of a garment. They are occasionally found at the waistline. When buying designer clothes, you are not only buying a quality garment, but also a piece of fashion history, which is sure to increase the garment's value.

Size is also important in determining the value of a garment. Extremely small or very large sizes are worth less than items of moderate sizes.

If you follow these simple guidelines, you should be able to purchase items suitable for your collection.

Fabric Glossary

Crepe has a wrinkled, rough, pebbly surface and is a name given to a variety of fabrics. Crepe was very popular during the 1930s and 1940s.

Batiste is a sheer lightweight fabric made of linen or cotton, used especially in lingerie and children's wear.

Broadcloth is a quality fabric with a compact texture and is made of cotton, nylon, wool, silk or blended fabrics. It has a napped and polished face.

Brocade is a weaved cloth made of silk or metallic yarn, or both, with a distinctive woven design.

Calico has a plain weave and is a medium-weight printed cotton with a smooth finish.

Cashmere is a soft, fluffy fabric woven or knitted, made from Kashmir goats' hair. Sometimes combined with wool, it is lightweight, warm, and expensive.

Chiffon is a sheer, soft, finely woven fabric mostly made of silk, and in later years, nylon. Chiffon was especially popular during the 1920s.

Corduroy is a durable, vertical-ribbed fabric, usually made of cotton. It was especially popular for riding habits and knickers around the turn of the century.

Felt is a dense, matted fabric of wool, fur, hair or cotton. Felt comes in a wide range of thicknesses and was a popular fabric for skirts during the 1950s.

Gabardine is a durable, woven worsted, popular especially in the 1930s through the 1950s.

Houndstooth is a broken-check weave fabric.

Jacquard is a group of fabrics with a large pattern-weave design.

Lamé is a group of fabrics with nontarnishable metallic threads, sometimes combined with other fabrics for various effects.

Lawn is a lightweight, plain-weave cotton with a crisp, crinkled finish.

Matelassé is a cotton or crepe fabric of double-cloth construction with raised and lowered motifs, providing a bright and dim effect.

Moiré is any fabric, especially faille, taffeta or organdy, with a wavy or watered look.

Muslin is a firm, durable, plain-weave cotton of various weights.

Organdy is a transparent cloth with a harsh feel, permanently starched and durable.

Organza is a nylon or silk plain-weave fabric, similar to cotton organdy.

Pique is a fine-textured cotton fabric having a vertical-ribbed effect. Other weaves include bird's-eye, honeycomb and waffle. Pique is very durable and easy to care for.

Plush is a pile cloth made from any fibers with a pile effect of more than ⅛ inch in height. It is used especially for capes and coats.

Pongee is a soft, plain-weave fabric of undyed wild silk and is easily identified by its irregular yarns. It was especially popular for men's shirts and ladies' robes.

Satin is a woven fabric with a lustrous face and dull back, made from silks, acetates, rayons, and other fabrics.

Serge is a twilled, clear-finish worsted with a cotton warp, made in a small-twill repeat design.

Shantung is a cotton cloth originally made of silk with a slub yarn effect in the warp or filling.

Sharkskin is a fine-textured worsted with a distinctive color-effect twill weave, popular in men's suits, especially in the 1950s.

Taffeta is a smooth, glossy, plain-weave silk, rayon, acetate or nylon, often with moiré finish.

Velvet is a thick pile cloth of silk, acetate, rayon or nylon, in which warp yarns are cut for pile effect.

Velveteen is a cotton-filling pile cloth with cut-filling yarns.

Voile is a very soft, sheer, plain-weave fabric usually made of cotton.

Worsted refers to any of a group of fabrics made from selected wool fibers that are carded and combed. Worsted yarns are uniform and smooth with parallel fibers. Worsteds have a higher texture than woolens and are lighter in weight.

A Guide to Fabrics

There are four major natural fibers: linen, cotton, silk and wool. These were basically the only fabrics used until the introduction of rayon in the 1920s.

Linen is a durable, absorbent fabric made from flax. It is smooth and strong with a fiber somewhat irregular when compared with cotton or silk. Linen was an especially popular fabric during the Victorian and Edwardian periods. It is rarely used today. When found, garments made of linen are very expensive.

Cotton was the most common fabric used for shirts, nightgowns, blouses and petticoats. It is made from the white fiber surrounding the seeds of the cotton plant. Cotton is also very durable, and the fibers are usually very regular.

Silk, a soft, luxurious fabric, is made of fibers spun by the silk moth caterpillar. It is a very delicate fabric and must be handled and stored with care to avoid deterioration.

Wool is a heavy, durable fabric that comes from sheep and other animals. It is a lovely fabric when woven into gabardine, which was especially popular in the late 1930s and early 1940s.

Other popular fabrics like rayon, acetate, and nylon are man-made. Acetate is wrinkle-resistant and often made into satins, taffetas, and sharkskins. Rayon on the other hand will wrinkle and shrink when washed. Dry cleaning is recommended. Many crepes, taffetas, velvets and gabardines are made of rayon.

Beadwork

Any clothing you come across with beadwork will be valued highly, as it is costly today to have anything beaded. Beadwork always makes a garment more attractive. The beads you will find on pre-1940 clothing are almost always made of glass or jet — wonderful, practical materials that do not melt when exposed to heat.

Beading was especially popular on Victorian dresses, bodices and capes. Beadwork as a trimming reached its peak in the 1920s, when row upon row of beads graced the colorful flapper evening dresses. Beaded flapper dresses are highly collectible today, especially if in excellent condition.

After the 1920s beadwork was still popular, but to a lesser degree. Some of the late 1930s and early 1940s blouses, dresses and suits may have beaded or sequined adornments. Beads and sequins on hats were extremely popular during the 1940s. And during the 1950s beaded sweaters became popular, with some beaded sweaters still being made today. These sweaters are collectible from a practical point of view. Most people buy them for wear.

Beaded purses have been popular since the eighteenth century, with their popularity peaking in the 1920s. While beaded purses can still be purchased today, the quality does not match that of the earlier pieces, which are popular collector items.

Caring for Vintage Clothing

One of the most important aspects of collecting or dealing in antique or vintage clothing is garment care, restoration and storage. Almost all vintage pieces will need a good airing, or cleaning, and possibly some repair. A word of caution: Remember that fabrics tend to become fragile with age, especially silk. Take care to clean your garments properly.

It is not advisable to wash any vintage garment in a washing machine or to dry it in a dryer. As fabrics age, they tend to become less durable, so careful hand washing is recommended for cottons and linens, and dry cleaning for wools, silks and synthetics.

Stains present a special problem. In silk, stains are almost impossible to remove, so beware. Stains in linen and cotton are easier to remove, sometimes with good results. Always hand wash your garments with a gentle detergent. For some stains or yellowing you may need to use a safety bleach. Be sure to follow the manufacturer's directions. While a garment is soaking, check the item frequently. The minute a garment is clean, remove it and rinse it well. As with all cotton, washing in cool water is suggested, as hot or warm water may shrink a garment.

For dark spots or rust stains, lemon and salt, a concoction that may be older than the garment itself, is an effective bleaching agent. Use one part lemon juice to one part water with a pinch of salt. Carefully dab the area with the solution and expose the garment to strong sunlight, if possible. Sometimes, for tiny spots on cotton or linen, dabbing with a bleach-soaked cotton swab may make stubborn spots disappear. But dab with bleach cautiously. If you notice the bleach fraying or rotting the fabric, stop.

Never wring washed items. Wringing can ruin the shape of your garment. To dry a garment effectively so that it retains its original shape, place it flat on a towel and let it dry naturally.

Beaded items need special care. Earlier garments, those made before 1940, can generally be dry-cleaned successfully, as most of the beads were made of glass or jet. Some of the later pieces, such as the beaded sweaters of the 1950s, have plastic beads, which may melt if not cleaned properly. Check with your dry cleaner for professional advice.

Care should be taken when pressing clothes, too. Steaming is always recommended. If you do not have a steamer, you may use your iron. But use it cautiously. Be sure to use the proper setting for the fabric you are pressing, according to directions on your iron. Cottons and linens should be ironed damp with a hot iron. To avoid fabric sheen, iron on the wrong side of the garment. Special attention should be given to trims and laces. Steaming is the best way to unwrinkle handmade laces, as ironing can ruin the natural pattern. Avoid running an iron over beadwork and buttons, especially

on newer items, which could be made of plastic. Synthetic fabrics generally take a much cooler iron.

Storing Vintage Clothing

Protect your investment by storing vintage clothing properly. Be sure a garment is clean before it is stored. Hanging is generally the best way to store clothing, excluding the fragile, heavily beaded dresses of the 1920s. Be sure the garment is equally distributed on the hanger to avoid stress at the shoulders. Tissue can be used to pad the shoulders.

Beaded dresses and delicate lingerie should be stored flat, wrapped in acid-free tissue paper, preferably in cardboard or wooden storage boxes. High humidity can damage fabrics, just as heat can. Therefore, plastic bags should not be used because of the condensation that may result. Clothing should never be stored in areas of high humidity or heat.

Making Money in the Collectible Clothing Business

Making money working with vintage clothing can be fun and easy with a minimal investment, a little time, and lots of knowledge. One of the easiest ways to earn a profit is to buy and sell to other dealers. Buying the clothing at a price that allows you *and* the dealer to make a profit is the key to success. Shopping at thrift stores, yard sales, and flea markets is one way to find interesting, yet inexpensive items.

Patience is also an important virtue. Do not be discouraged if a dealer is not interested in buying all you have to offer. Different dealers will buy different items. A dealer knows what he can sell. Most dealers will pay one-third to one-half of a garment's retail price to allow for adequate profit. Bear in mind that a dealer has rent, utilities, and other expenses to pay before he can make a profit, not to mention the fact that it might take months for the right buyer to come along to buy a particular garment.

Most dealers are particular about the condition and sizes of the garments they choose to place on their racks, and justifiably so. No one wants to wear or buy worn, repaired, or stained garments. Do you?

Dealers on the other hand should extend certain courtesies to those trying to sell them garments. As a wholesaler, I have met many a dealer who expected to buy clothing from me at a thrift store price, which is unreasonable. Boxes of garments sent to dealers on approval should be quickly reviewed, with any returns or payment for merchandise kept sent immediately. Dealers should feel proud that someone trusts them enough to extend them this courtesy.

If you do not care to function as a wholesaler, yet you have an itch to open your own little shop, do so. This takes a larger investment and will probably require more of your time. Your success will depend largely on your location and your ability to deal with people.

For the creative seamstress, there are unlimited opportunities in the vintage clothing business. Seamstresses who are capable of restoring antique pieces are in demand and can just about set their own price. Laces and old fabrics can be worked into lovely remakes of old-fashioned styles, then sold at boutiques or specialty shops. One woman I know now sells her lacy reproductions to several major chain stores. So you see, with a little incentive and creativity, you can start a profitable business of your own dealing in vintage clothes.

Where to Buy Vintage Clothing

The vintage clothing business is big in the United States, and growing. New stores are opening as the trend toward collecting old clothes increases in popularity.

Although many people are becoming wise to the great demand for vintage pieces, many are still unaware of their value. Therefore, items can still be found at thrift stores, yard sales, and flea markets across the country. Estate sales and auctions are good places to look, too. Heirloom pieces are still found in many attics and basements.

It is also possible to purchase clothing by advertising in your local newspaper. Try to word your advertisement in a way that will appeal to the general public. Many people have not even heard the term *vintage clothing* and may not know what you are referring to. It might be better to word your advertisement, "Wanted: antique clothing, 1880 to 1960," or something similar to this.

Another route you might take is to purchase clothing through the mail. There are many mail-order dealers who regularly advertise in national antique newspapers. If you decide to buy by mail, be sure that you have return privileges, otherwise you easily could get burned. If you do purchase garments through the mail, and you are not satisfied, return the items promptly and in the condition they were in when you received them. It is customary in the mail-order business for the purchaser to pay the shipping charges, *both ways*.

The best place to go to find quality vintage clothing is to one of the many specialty stores located throughout the United States. The shops carry quality garments that have been properly restored and are ready to wear. Most shops provide a comfortable and nostalgic atmosphere. The prices will be higher in a shop than at a thrift store, of course, but at least the vintage pieces will have been cleaned and restored.

There are dozens of excellent vintage clothing stores across the United States. Regrettably, I cannot list all of them. I would suggest that you check your local telephone directory for shops in your area. Look under "Antiques," "Boutiques," "Women's Apparel," or "Second-Hand Stores."

If you would like to have your store listed in an updated edition of this book, write to me at Wallace-Homestead Book Company or at P.O. Box 835, Pueblo, Colorado 81002.

Antique and Vintage Clothing Stores

Arizona

Scottsdale

Chic to Chaps
10610 71st Place
Scottsdale, Arizona 85254
    Western and English riding clothes.

Dynabelles
3704 N. Scottsdale Road
Scottsdale, Arizona 85251
    Victorian through 1950s quality clothing.

Ye Olde Curiosity Shoppe
7245 E. First Avenue
Scottsdale, Arizona 85251
    1880 bridal dresses, fur coats, jewelry.

Tucson

How Sweet It Was
636 N. 4th Avenue
Tucson, Arizona 85705

California

Albany

Second Hand Rose
1111 Solano Avenue
Albany, California 94706
Collectible clothing and accessories,
jewelry, furs.

Beverly Hills

Camp Beverly Hills
9640 Little Santa Monica Boulevard
Beverly Hills, California 90210
Military surplus, Hawaiian and
bowling shirts.

Clovis

Clovis Collectables
606 4th Street
Clovis, California 93612
Pre-1940 vintage clothing.

Hollywood

Junk for Joy
5065 Lankershim Boulevard
North Hollywood, California 91601
Kimonos, halloween costumes, store
stock, vintage clothing.

West End Clothing
7982 Santa Monica Boulevard
West Hollywood, California 90046
Men's and ladies' pre-1950 clothing,
rhinestone and lucite jewelry.

Larkspur

Shadows of Forgotten Ancestors
503 Magnolia
Larkspur, California 94939
White lace clothing from 1900 to 1920,
folk costumes.

Jackson

Fallon Trading Company
5 Main Street, Upstairs
Jackson, California 95642
Victorian through 1940s clothing,
shoes, hats and furs.

Los Angeles

A Store is Born
727 N. La Brea
Los Angeles, California 90038
Vintage apparel for men and women,
including hats, shoes, and costume
jewelry. Costume rentals.

Crystal Palace
8435 Melrose Avenue
Los Angeles, California 90069
Quality antique clothing.

Stella Goldstein
1102 S. La Cienega Boulevard
Los Angeles, California 90035
Specializing in nearly new and vintage
furs, costumes, and designer clothing.

Oakland

Bizarre Bazaar
5634 College Avenue
Oakland, California 94618
Victorian through 1950s clothing,
costuming.

Old Pasadena

Somewhere In Time
26 S. Raymond Avenue
Old Pasadena, California 91105
Graceful antique and vintage clothing.

Pasadena

Lee's Gingerbread
17 South Sierra Madre Boulevard
Pasadena, California 91107

San Diego

Buffalo Breath
1451 Garnet Avenue
San Diego, California 92109
  Quality vintage clothing and costume rentals.

Chic to Chic
4880 Cass Street
San Diego, California 92109
  Quality vintage clothing.

Mixed Produce
1475 University Avenue
San Diego, California 92103
  Ladies' clothing, 1920 to 1950, men's clothing, 1940 to 1950s. Art Deco costume jewelry.

Special Effects
3822 Fourth Avenue
San Diego, California 92103
  Men's and women's vintage clothing and accessories.

Wear It Again Sam
3922 Park Boulevard
San Diego, California 92103
  Ladies' Victorian to 1950 quality clothing. Men's vintage clothing and accessories.

Yesteryears Clothing
5054 Newport Avenue
Ocean Beach
San Diego, California 92107
  Vintage clothing.

Sunnyvale

Alyce's Costume Corner
167 E. Fremont Avenue
Sunnyvale, California 94087
  Antique clothing, costume rental, consignments.

Tustin

Ginny's Antiques, Et Ct, Inc.
190 El Camino Real
Tustin, California 92680
  Quality vintage clothing.

San Francisco

Masquerade
2237 Union Street
San Francisco, California 94123
  Quality ladies' and men's vintage clothing, 1890 to 1950.

Matinee
1124 Polk Street
San Francisco, California 94109
  Vintage clothing, 1800 to present.

Notorious
1388 Haight Street
San Francisco, California 94117
  Victorian to 1940 quality vintage clothing, accessories, and jewelry.

Old Gold
2380 Market Street
San Francisco, California 94114
  Men's and women's vintage clothing, 1920 to 1960.

Second Hand Rose
3326 23rd Street
San Francisco, California 94110
  Collectible clothing and accessories, jewelry, furs.

Colorado

Boulder

The Ritz
949 Walnut Street
Boulder, Colorado 80302
  Vintage clothing and accessories, 1920 to 1960.

Colorado Springs

The Flamingo
2427 W. Colorado Avenue
Colorado Springs, Colorado 80904
  Vintage clothing and accessories.

Denver

Nostalgia Shop
2431 S. University
Denver, Colorado 80218
  1930s and 1940s vintage clothing.

Rudely Decadent
1388 S. Broadway
Denver, Colorado 80210
   1930s to present vintage clothing, new
   wave.

Connecticut
Newington

The Doll Factory
2551 Berlin Turnpike
Newington, Connecticut 06111
   Men's and ladies' quality vintage
   clothing, specializing in beaded items,
   stage and theatrical clothing, furs.

Florida
St. Augustine

Pamela's Reminiscence
14 D St. George Street
St. Augustine, Florida 32084
   1800s to 1950 quality vintage clothing.

Georgia
Atlanta

Puttin' on the Ritz
3099 Peachtree Road NE
Atlanta, Georgia 30305
   Quality antique clothing, 1800s to
   1950s.

Savannah

Tilley's
20 W. Harris Street
Savannah, Georgia 31401
   Quality pre-1950s clothing,
   specializing in Victorian bridal and ball
   gowns.

Illinois
Chicago

Clark St. Waltz
2360 N. Lincoln Avenue
Chicago, Illinois 60614
   Victorian to 1950 vintage clothing,
   kimonos.

Divine Idea
2959 N. Clark
Chicago, Illinois 60657
   Never worn and slightly used clothing
   from 1950s and 1960s.

Dream Weaver
835 W. Webster Avenue
Chicago, Illinois 60614
   1940s and 1950s clothing and hats.

Second Childhood
5734 N. Glenwood
Chicago, Illinois 60660
   Antique christening dresses.

Silver Moon
3337 N. Halsted
Chicago, Illinois 60657

Naperville

Yesterday and Today Shop
209 S. Washington Street
Naperville, Illinois 60540
   Victorian and turn of the century
   clothing.

Indiana
Historic Madison

Walkers North Bank Antiques
319 Jefferson Street
Historic Madison, Indiana 47250
   Victorian clothing, purses, and
   accessories.

Iowa
Davenport

Trash Can Annie
421 Brady Street
Davenport, Iowa 52801
   Victorian through 1940s clothing,
   wedding gowns, and embroidered
   kimonos.

Kentucky
Louisville

The Cubby Hole
1420 Bardstown
Louisville, Kentucky 40205
   1800s to 1950s clothing and
   accessories.

Louisiana
New Orleans

Matilda
1222 Decatur
New Orleans, Louisiana
   Ladies' and men's vintage clothing,
   Mardi Gras costumes.

Second Hand Rose
3110 Magazine and 1129 Decatur
New Orleans, Louisiana 70115
   Quality vintage clothing, 1850 to 1950.

Maine

Richmond

The Loft
9 Gardiner Street
Richmond, Maine 04357
   Antique clothing and lace.

Massachusetts

Boston

Bluefingers
101 Charles Street, Beacon Hill
Boston, Massachusetts 02114
   Civil War to 1960s clothing, New
   England Victorian garments, Japanese
   antique kimonos, fur coats.

Forever Flamingo
285 Newbury Street
Boston, Massachusetts 02115
   1930s to 1950s vintage men's and
   women's clothing.

Brookline

Zazu: Fashions with a Past
395A Harvard Street
Brookline, Massachusetts 02146
   Men's and women's vintage fashions.

Cambridge

Great Eastern Trading Company, Inc.
49 River Street
Cambridge, Massachusetts 02139
   Men's and women's vintage clothing
   and accessories.

Vintage, Etc.
2014A Massachusetts Avenue
Cambridge, Massachusetts 02140
   Quality clothing from 1940 through
   1950s.

Great Barrington

Down Home
173 Main
Great Barrington, Massachusetts 01230
   Victorian whites, hats, and shoes.

Michigan

Okimas

My Wife's Antiques
3944 Meridian Road
Okimas, Michigan 48864
   Pre-1940 clothing.

Royal Oak

Patti Smith
511 S. Washington
Royal Oak, Michigan 48067
   Victorian through 1950s men's and
   women's clothing and accessories.

Missouri

St. Louis

Nostalgia Boutique
1 S. Euclid
St. Louis, Missouri 63108
   1890 through 1950s vintage clothing,
   accessories, furs.

Nevada

Las Vegas

Garbo's
3585 S. Maryland Parkway, Suite F
Las Vegas, Nevada 89109
   Vintage and antique clothing.

New Jersey

Rutherford

Studio I — Marguerite Morgan
6 Highland Cross
Rutherford, New Jersey 07070
   Antique lace, antique and vintage
   clothing, restoration.

New York

Albany

The Albany Collection
297 Hamilton Street
Albany, New York 12210
   Edwardian and Victorian white
   dresses.

Glendale Queens

Vintage Vogue, Ltd.
65-22 Myrtle Avenue
Glendale Queens, New York 11385
   Vintage clothing.

Glenwood Landing

Nanny's Attic
129 Glenwood Road
Glenwood Landing, New York 11547
  1900-1950 ladies' and men's clothing
  and accessories, tuxedos and tails.

Kingston

Outback Antiques
72 Hurley Avenue
Kingston, New York 12401
  Antique and vintage clothing for men
  and women, lace.

New York City

Cherchez
864 Lexington
New York, New York 10021
  Victorian clothing, Chinese
  embroideries and paisley shawls.

Fondas
168 Lexington Avenue
New York, New York 10016

Fondas
346 East 59th Street
New York, New York 10022
  Victorian blouses and wedding
  gowns, 1930 through 1960s, clothing
  and accessories. Beaded 1920s dresses.

Halina's Boutique
160 West 55th Street
New York, New York 10019
  Antique hair combs, marcasite jewelry.

Havona Designs, Inc.
110 Thompson Street
New York, New York 10012
  Quality vintage clothing, costumes.

One Woman
336 Columbus Avenue, 76th Street
New York, New York 10023
  Victorian white clothing, 1940s
  clothing, vintage furs.

Pentimenti
126 Prince Street
New York, New York 10012
  Victorian through 1940s quality
  clothing. Hand-embroidered Chinese
  piano shawls, Art Deco metal on
  gauze shawls.

Richard Utilla
112 Christopher Street
New York, New York 10014

Richard Utilla
324 Bleecker Street
New York, New York 10014
  Large variety of quality vintage
  clothing, costuming.

Screaming Mimi's
100 West 83 Street
New York, New York 10024
  Men's and women's clothing, 1940s
  through 1950s, shoes, tuxedos.

Somethin Else
182 Ninth Avenue
New York, New York 10011
  Victorian clothing.

Victoria Falls
147 Spring Street
New York, New York 10012
  Victorian white clothing, 1920s quality
  clothing. Some unusual 1930s through
  1950s clothing, costumes.

Saratoga Springs

Mariposa
20 Caroline Street
Saratoga Springs, New York 12866
  Victorian whites, bridal wear.

Ohio

Cincinnati

Scentiments
2614 Vine Street
Cincinnati, Ohio 45219
  Men's and women's vintage clothing,
  1920s through 1960s, new wave
  clothing, accessories.

Downtown
119 Calhoun Street
Cincinnati, Ohio 45219
  Vintage clothing for men, women,
  and children from 1920 through 1950.

Cleveland Heights

Belladonna
1834 Coventry Road 6
Cleveland Heights, Ohio 44118
  Vintage clothing, furs, and jewelry.

Lakewood

Flashback
1392 Bonnieview Avenue
Lakewood, Ohio 44107
    Quality vintage clothing and jewelry.

Oregon

Portland

Bohemia
219 SW 6th, Portland Mall
Portland, Oregon 97204
    1900 to 1940 clothing, jewelry.

Cal's Books and Wares
732 SW 1st
Portland, Oregon 97204
    Victorian through 1950s clothing.

Nancy's Antiques
8522 SE 17th (Sellwood area)
Portland, Oregon 97202
    Vintage clothing.

Pennsylvania

Pittsburgh

Club Anonymous
284 Morewood Avenue (Shadyside)
Pittsburgh, Pennsylvania 15213
    Quality ladies' and men's vintage
    apparel from 1850 to 1960.

Yesterday's News
538 Brownsville Road
Pittsburgh, Pennsylvania 15227
    Men's and ladies' quality clothing,
    1900 to 1960, accessories, jewelry, and
    furs.

Texas

Austin

Waterloo Compound Antiques
600 East Third
Austin, Texas 78767
    Vintage clothing, specializing in
    evening wear.

Houston

Flashback
2502 Ralph
Houston, Texas 77006
    Ladies' and men's vintage clothing,
    1930 through 1950s, most are unworn,
    accessories, jewelry.

Montage
3632 University Boulevard
Houston, Texas 77005
    Top quality Victorian and Edwardian
    white dresses, blouses, lingerie.

Yesterday's Rose
452 W. 19th Street
Houston, Texas 77008
    Low-priced wearable clothing and
    accessories.

Utah

Salt Lake City

Arsenic and Old Lace
407 E. 3rd South
Salt Lake City, Utah 84111
    Vintage clothing from 1860 to 1950,
    lace, buttons.

Don T. Davidson Plantique
2804 S. State
Salt Lake City, Utah 84115
    Old clothes, hats, accessories.

Remember When
251 S. State
Salt Lake City, Utah 84111
    Vintage clothing and accessories.

Virginia

Roanoke

Jezebel's
105 Market Square
Roanoke, Virginia 24011
    Antique and vintage clothing from
    1890 to 1960, accessories.

Washington

Seattle

Dreamland
619 Broadway East
Seattle, Washington 98102

Dreamland
1905 3rd Avenue
Seattle, Washington 98102
    Vintage clothing and accessories.

Grandma's Attic
Pike Place Market
2 Level 319
Seattle, Washington 98101
    Men's and women's vintage clothing
    and accessories.

Out of the Past
219 Broadway East
Seattle, Washington 98102
  Vintage clothing.

Vintage Clothing
6501 Roosevelt NE
Seattle, Washington 98116
  Quality men's, women's and
  children's clothing and accessories,
  pre-1950.

Washington, D.C.
Georgetown

Off the Cuff, Ltd.
1077 Wisconsin Avenue, NW
Georgetown, Washington, D.C. 20007
  Antique kimonos, jewelry, handmade
  lace, antique blouses.

Jameson and Hawkins
3061½ M Street, NW
Georgetown, Washington, D.C. 20007
  1900 to 1955 quality wedding,
  evening, and designer dresses.

Over Flow II
1226 Wisconsin Avenue, NW
Georgetown, Washington, D.C. 20007
  Men's and women's quality antique
  apparel and costumes.

Accessories

Collecting accessories is exciting because of their diversity. Whether you collect purses, hats, fans, combs, or all of these, the possibilities for adding new pieces to your collection or wardrobe are endless. Most accessories are relatively inexpensive and make wonderful gifts.

Miscellaneous

Cambric apron, c. 1871, from Victorian Fashions and Costumes from Harper's Bazar, 1867-1898, **$20-30.**

Scarlet grosgrain cravat bow, c. 1871, from Victorian Fashions and Costumes from Harper's Bazar, 1867-1898, **$10-15.**

Silk shoe rosette with flowers, c. 1871, from Victorian Fashions and Costumes from Harper's Bazar, 1867-1898, **$8-10.**

Tortoiseshell comb and hairpins, c. 1887, from Victorian Fashions and Costumes from Harper's Bazar, 1867-1898, **$70-90 each.**

Parasols, c. 1870, from Victorian Fashions and Costumes, **$80-110 each.**

Swiss muslin collar with lace insertion and lace fichu, c. 1871, from Victorian Fashions and Costumes from Harper's Bazar, 1867-1898, **$20-35.**

Cloth walking boots and kid carriage shoe, c. 1882, from Victorian Fashions and Costumes, **$50-70 each.**

Silk cord agrafe, with tassels, c. 1870, from Victorian Fashions and Costumes, **$5-15.**

Fan, hand painted, c. 1800-1825, **$200-220.**

Fan, hand painted and signed "T. Houghton," c. 1870-1890, **$225-250.**

Collar, black lace, high neck, c. 1890-1900, **$8-10.**

Collar box, papier-maché, celluloid inset, c. 1880-1895, **$30-40.**

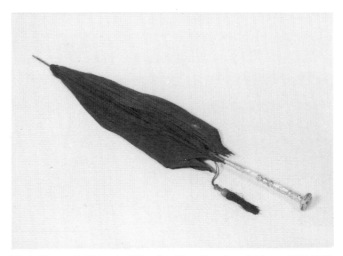

Black silk parasol, 14-karat gold handle with mother-of-pearl inlay, c. 1880-1900,
$80-90.

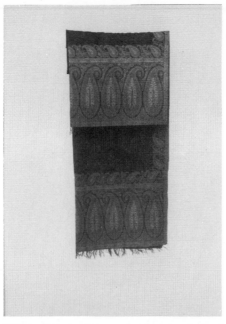

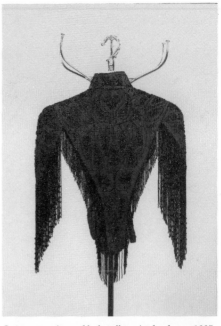

Large, square, woven paisley shawl, shades of red, numbered 97995, c. 1880-1900, **$150-175.**

Woven paisley shawl, long and rectangular, shades of gray and black, c. 1880-1900, **$130-160.**

Corsage garniture, black taffeta, jet beads, c. 1885-1900, **$125-150.**

Fan, white feathers on ivory celluloid sticks, c. 1890-1900, **$80-100.**

White silk fan, hand painted, wooden sticks, c. 1890-1900, **$50-60.**

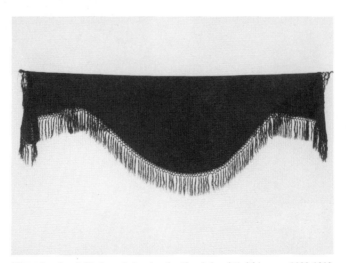

Mourning shawl, black wool, hand-embroidered, hand-tied fringe, c. 1890-1910, **$80-90.**

Blue and white striped silk vest, c. 1890-1900, **$15-20.**

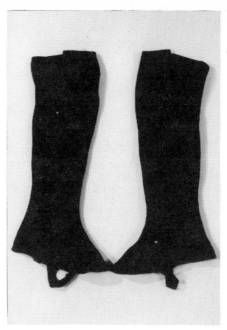

Leggins, knee length, black wool, never worn, c. 1900-1910, **$20-25.**

Apron, white cotton, full length, c. 1900-1910, **$12-15.**

Fan, clipped ostrich feathers, celluloid sticks, c. 1895-1910, **$70-80.**

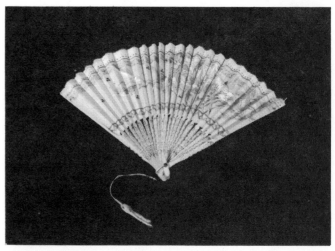

Fan, hand painted pastel flowers on white linen, c. 1900-1905, **$40-50.**

High-top shoes, lace-up style, black leather, never worn, c. 1900-1910, **$40-50.**

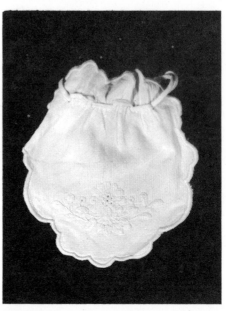

Bag with white hand-embroidery on white linen, drawstring, c. 1910-1920, **$20-25.**

Extra Quality Bridal Wreath, 85 Cents.

No. 39R289 Bridal Wreath, extra quality; well made wax orange blossoms, including brooch and bouquet, rubber stemming; if you pay $3.00 elsewhere you get no better.
Price, $1.65

No. 39R291 Bridal Wreath with brooch and bouquet made of wax orange blossoms. Why pay extravagant prices elsewhere? Price, each, 85c

No. 39R293 Elegant Straight Quills, imitation of the fine eagle quills; look and wear just as well, very popular and dressy. Length about 12 to 14 inches. Black or white. Price, each........................6c

No. 39R295 Pretty, broad quills, nice large size, special selected stock. Square cut top. as per illustration. Colors, black or white. Price, each..4c

Angel Wings.

No. 39R297 Angel Wings. This is a padded wing that always retails at 50 cents. Colors, black, white, brown or navy. Price, per pair..........16c

No. 39R299 Angel Wings, same shape as above. Larger size; better quality. Colors, black or white. Price, per pair.........33c

Stylish Aigrettes.

No. 39R301 Sweeping Paradise Aigrettes, long full feathers, six stems. A very handsome ornament. Colors, black or white. Price, each......50c

No. 39R303 Handsome Jetted Black Ostrich Aigrette, a full, rich trimming for hats. Black only. Price, each...................22c

Black Parrots, 45 Cents.

No. 39R305 Fine Selected Quality Black Parrots, rich, glossy and full length. Price. 45c

No. 39R307 Black Feather Breast, which will be especially good on turbans as well as on hats. Splendid value. Black and white. Price, each..................25c

No. 39R309 Pretty Feather Breasts, much larger and fuller than above. Breasts this season we highly recommend as a fashionable trimming, and this number is exceptional value. Colors, black, white and brown. Price, each....................48c

No. 39R311 Fancy Black Jetted Coque Feather, a stylish and showy trimming at a very low price. A trifle less perhaps than your home dealer pays for them at wholesale. Price, each................13c

Jetted Aigrettes.

No. 39R313 Jetted Aigrette to be used in connection with other trimming, and very good on bonnets. Price, each..............10c

Assorted hat trims advertised in the 1904 Sears, Roebuck & Co. Catalogue, $5-15 each.

Blue ostrich boa, c. 1910-1925, $35-50.

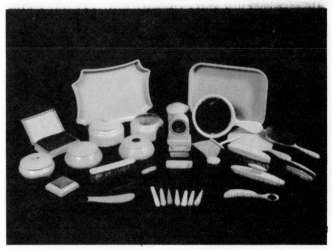

Celluloid dresser set, assorted pieces, c. 1910, $150-170.

Fan, peacock feathers, hand-carved teakwood sticks, c. 1910, $75-90.

Fan, oriental, hand painted, hand-carved teakwood sticks, c. 1910-1925, **$50-60.**

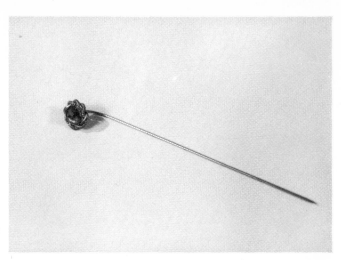

Hatpin, brass with lavender glass inset, c. 1910-1920, **$12-15.**

Chinese shawl, large square, white silk, hand-embroidered, hand-tied fringe, c. 1910-1925, **$250-275.**

Black silk shoes, cut steel and jet beads, some wear, c. 1910-1920, **$25-40.**

Black silk and leather shoes, hand-etched sterling silver buckles, c. 1910-1920, **$40-45.**

French shawl, machine woven, gray silk, c. 1918, **$35-40.**

Flapper beads, turquoise, red, and brown, c. 1920-1930, **$35-40.**

Flapper beads, crocheted blue carnival glass beads, c. 1920-1930, **$40-45.**

Black celluloid buffer, enameled floral inset, c. 1920-1930, **$10-12.**

Capelet, brown ostrich feathers, c. 1920-1930, **$45-50.**

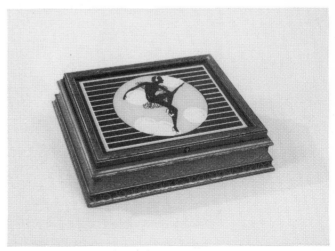

Dresser box, reverse painted by hand on glass and wood, Art Deco, c. 1920-1930, **$50-60.**

Dresser box, reverse painted by hand on glass and wood, Art Deco, c. 1920-1930, **$50-60.**

Fan, paper and lacquered wooden sticks, hand painted, c. 1920, **$45-55.**

Fan, paper and lacquered wooden sticks, hand painted oriental style, c. 1920-1930, **$65-80.**

Fan, linen with enameled wooden sticks, hand painted, c. 1920-1930, **$40-50.**

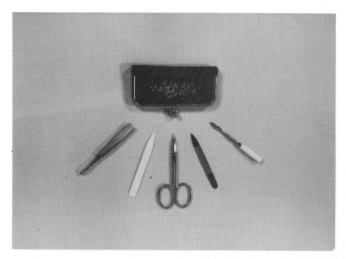

Manicure set, suede and embroidered case, celluloid and metal accessories, c. 1920-1930, **$20-30.**

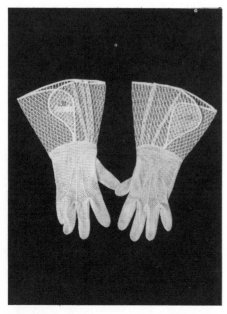

White cotton net gloves, never worn, c. 1920-1930, **$20-25.**

Wool gloves, Art Deco style, never worn, c. 1920-1930, **$20-25.**

Oriental tea parasol, brown and white hand painted, paper, c. 1920-1930, **$40-50.**

Rouge cases, never used, c. 1920-1930, **$5-6 each.**

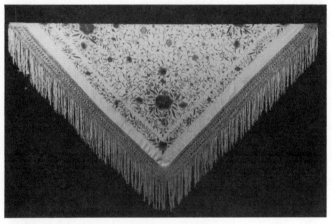

Spanish shawl, large square, shades of orange, flower hand-embroidery on white silk, hand-tied fringe, c. 1920-1930, **$100-150.**

Long rectangular shawl, black silk, c. 1920-1930, **$35-45.**

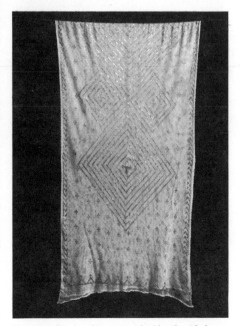

Egyptian shawl, white net embroidered with brass, rectangular, c. 1920-1930, **$70-100.**

Black suede shoes, c. 1920-1930, **$35-40.**

Shoes, white kid leather, never worn, c. 1920-1930, **$50-60.**

35

Black silk shoes, gold metallic leather, c. 1920-1930, **$35-40.**

Black leather pumps, French heels, never worn, c. 1920-1930, **$45-50.**

Collar button, Italian mosaic, c. 1925-1935, **$15-20.**

Powder boxes, never used, c. 1925-1930, **$7-12 each.**

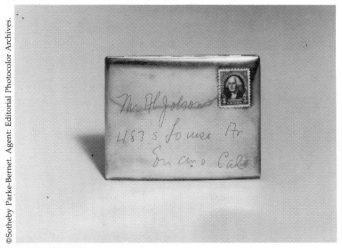

Silver cigarette case, fashioned as an envelope engraved with the name and address of Mr. Al Jolson, enameled in blue and white with a three-cent stamp, c. 1925-1930, **$1,000-1,400.**

Fan, oriental orange and peach silk, hand painted, wooden sticks, c. 1930-1940, **$25-30.**

36

Gloves, black suede, elbow length, c. 1930-1940, **$25-30.**

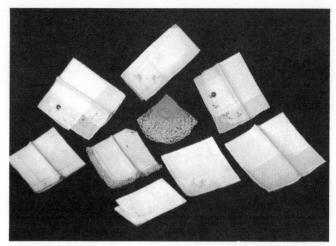

Handkerchiefs, linen and silk, never used, c. 1930-1935, **$1-3 each.**

White metal cigarette case, with thumbpiece ornament of faux sapphires, set in gold, black suede handled folder, c. 1930-1940, **$500-700.**

White celluloid fan, airbrushed flowers, c. 1935-1945, **$20-25.**

White and gold leather pumps, c. 1930-1935, **$40-45.**

Black silk gloves, shirred, c. 1940-1945, **$15-20.**

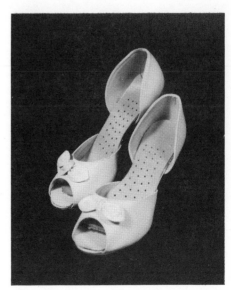

Shoes, white leather, high heels, never worn, c. 1940-1950, **$25-35.**

Shoes, high heels, navy polished leather, never worn, c. 1940, **$25-35.**

Sunglasses, black, red and white striped plastic, dark green lenses, stamped "Claire McCardell," c. 1950-1960, **$125-150.**

Shoes, cobra skin, c. 1955-1960, **$20-25.**

Shoes, high heels, brown dyed lizard, c. 1960-1965, **$20-30.**

Combs

Comb, black gutta-percha, c. 1870-1885, **$80-90.**

Comb, black gutta-percha, c. 1870-1890, **$75-85.**

Comb, tortoiseshell with 18-karat gold overlay, c. 1880-1900, **$125-135.**

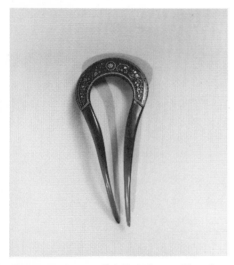

Chignon pin, brown celluloid, 18-karat gold overlay, c. 1890-1900, **$60-70.**

Comb, black gutta-percha, Art Nouveau style, c. 1890-1900, **$70-80.**

Black gutta-percha comb, jet insets, c. 1890-1900, **$75-90.**

Comb, tortiseshell with inlaid rhinestones, c. 1890-1900, **$70-80.**

Marbled celluloid chignon pin, c. 1900-1910, **$15-20.**

Comb, yellow celluloid, blue rhinestones, hand carved, c. 1900-1915, **$40-50.**

Comb, simulated tortiseshell, celluloid, c. 1910-1920, **$35-40.**

Comb, pink celluloid, red rhinestones, c. 1910-1920, **$45-50.**

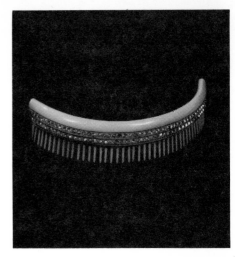

Pompadour comb, white celluloid, c. 1915-1930, **$25-30.**

Chignon pin, celluloid and sterling silver, c. 1920-1930, **$30-40.**

Black celluloid chignon pick, c. 1920-1930, **$15-20.**

Comb, black celluloid, c. 1920-1930, **$20-25.**

Comb, black enamel on yellow celluloid, c. 1920-1930, **$40-50.**

Comb, black enamel on yellow celluloid, c. 1920-1930, **$55-65.**

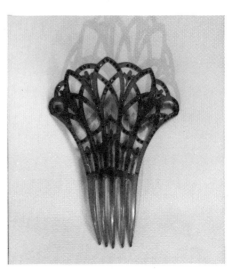

Clear red celluloid comb, red rhinestones, c. 1920-1930, **$45-55.**

Blue celluloid comb, hand-painted gold designs, c. 1920-1930, **$40-45.**

Comb, black enamel on yellow celluloid, c. 1920-1930, **$30-35.**

Pompadour comb, blue enamel on clear celluloid, blue rhinestones, c. 1920-1930, **$35-45.**

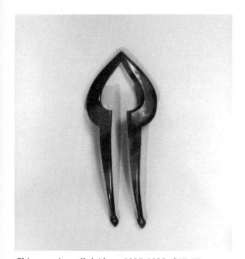

Chignon pin, celluloid, c. 1925-1930, **$15-17.**

Black celluloid barrette, white rhinestones, hand painted, c. 1930-1940, **$15-17.**

Clear celluloid chignon pin, white rhinestones, c. 1930-1940, **$12-15.**

Headband, black plastic, c. 1950-1960, **$8-10.**

Hats

Mourning hat, black knit, silk, c. 1870-1880, **$50-55.**

Black silk and lace mourning hat, hand-beaded with jet beads, c. 1870-1885, **$55-60.**

Mourning hat, black straw with cotton lace veil, c. 1870-1890, **$90-100.**

Mourning hat, beaver embroidered with piping, c. 1870-1890, **$90-100.**

Mourning hat, jet beads, ostrich plume on silk, c. 1870-1885, **$75-80.**

White cotton bonnet, handmade lace, c. 1880-1890, **$25-35.**

Dress hat, black velvet with yellow embroidery, c. 1880-1890, **$50-60.**

Black straw dress hat, c. 1880-1890, **$45-50.**

Dress hat, pink pleated silk and velvet, c. 1880-1895, **$70-80.**

Dress hat, black lace and silk with gold lamé, c. 1880-1890, **$50-55.**

Dress hat, black velvet and floral brocade, c. 1880-1890, **$60-70.**

Black silk mourning bonnet, c. 1880-1900, **$20-25.**

Mourning bonnet, black silk, c. 1880-1890, **$20-25.**

Dress hat, pastel silks and florals, c. 1885-1895, **$80-85.**

Bonnet, white pinstripe cotton, lace trim, c. 1890-1900, **$40-50.**

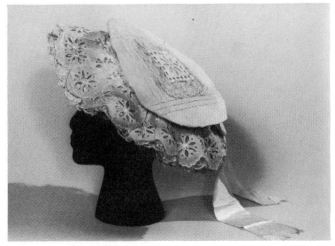

French bonnet, white cotton, trimmed with eyelet, lace and tucks, silk ribbons, c. 1890-1905, **$80-90.**

Dress hat, beige felt with brown ostrich plumes, c. 1890-1900, **$50-60.**

Dress hat, brown velvet with multicolored silk flowers, c. 1890-1900, **$50-60.**

Dress hat, black velvet with pastel silk flowers, c. 1890-1900, **$80-90.**

Dress hat, straw with velvet trim, c. 1890-1900, **$50-60.**

Black felt dress hat, velvet trim, ostrich plumes, c. 1890-1900, **$45-50.**

Beige velvet dress hat, ostrich plume, c. 1890-1900, **$75-80.**

Dress hat, black silk satin with an ostrich plume, c. 1890-1900, **$45-50.**

Dress hat, white felt with pink silk trim, c. 1890-1900, **$70-80.**

Black silk mourning hat, c. 1890-1900, **$25-30.**

Black felt mourning hat, c. 1890-1900, **$60-70.**

Straw sun hat, white and blue cotton print, c. 1890-1910, **$40-50.**

Black velvet dress hat, white silk, c. 1900-1910, **$70-75.**

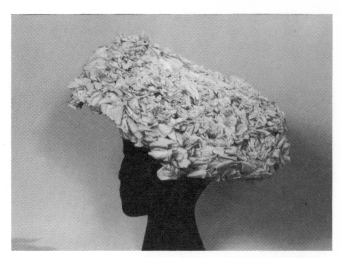

Yellow straw dress hat, ecru lace rose applique, silk ribbons, cotton miniature daisies, c. 1900-1910, **$75-100.**

White dress hat, silk daisies with yellow centers, c. 1900-1915, **$50-60.**

Wide-brimmed hat, brown velvet and plumes, c. 1900-1910, **$90-100.**

Black straw wide-brimmed hat, silk flowers, c. 1900-1910, **$90-100.**

Hats for late autumn, pictured in the November 1904 issue of The Designer, **$80-90 each.**

Brown velvet wide-brimmed hat, c. 1900-1910, **$75-80.**

White linen golf cap, c. 1910-1920, **$20-30.**

Cloche, lamé and beadwork on silk, c. 1920-1930, **$30-35.**

Cloche, peach net, pastel and lace appliques, c. 1920-1930, **$35-40.**

Mourning cloche, black straw and velvet, c. 1920-1930, **$15-20.**

Blue felt cloche, c. 1920-1930, **$25-30.**

Cloche, beige straw with pastel flowers, c. 1920-1930, **$40-45.**

Cloche, blue straw and velvet, white lace trim, c. 1920-1930, **$35-40.**

Skull cap, burgundy velvet, jet beads, c. 1920-1930, **$40-50.**

Rubber swim cap, c. 1920-1930, **$15-20.**

Dress hat, black straw, c. 1930-1940, **$5-10.**

Wide-brimmed straw hat, white with black rayon ribbon trim, c. 1930-1940, **$30-35.**

Yellow straw wide-brimmed hat, c. 1930-1940, **$25-30.**

Designer hat by Lilly Daché, black straw decorated with black feathers. Label reads "Lilly Daché — Paris — New York — 78 East 56th Street, NY," c. 1935-1945, **$280-300.**

Designer hat by Lilly Daché, pink satin and black suede, sewn overall with large square rhinestones, two matching hatpins. Label reads "Lilly Daché — Paris — New York — 78 East 56th Street, NY," c. 1935-1945, **$40-50.**

Dress hat, black felt, pink silk flowers, c. 1935-1940, **$15-20.**

Blue straw dress hat, c. 1935-1945, **$40-45.**

Black straw dress hat, c. 1935-1945, **$10-12.**

Wide-brimmed hat, rust straw, c. 1940-1945, **$40-50.**

Wide-brimmed hat, black straw with pink silk flowers, c. 1940-1945, **$25-30.**

Ecru dress hat, finely woven straw, chiffon overlay, pink chiffon flowers, c. 1940-1945, **$30-40.**

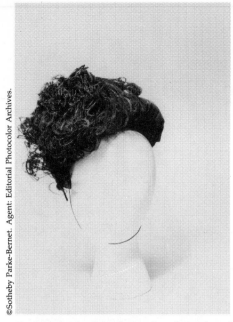

Dress hat, black velvet and satin, c. 1945-1950, **$8-10.**

Designer hat by Balenciaga, ruby velvet trimmed with black ostrich feathers. Label reads "Balenciaga — D — Avenue Georges V — Paris," c. 1950-1955, **$100-110.**

Purses

Grosgrain bag, c. 1881, from Victorian Fashions and Costumes, **$40-45.**

Plush bag, c. 1881, from Victorian Fashions and Costumes, **$50-55.**

Black crocheted purse, silk lining, cut steel beaded monogram, Art Nouveau twist-open top, c. 1900-1910, **$35-40.**

Silver-plated mount set with amethysts, with design of putti musicians among grapevines, c. 1900, **$120-140.**

Beaded purse, cut steel on leather, silver-plated Art Nouveau frame, belt clip, c. 1905-1915, **$100-110.**

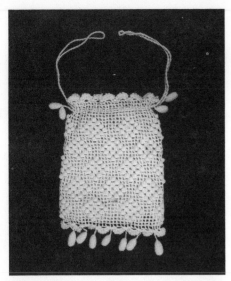

White on pink silk crocheted purse, c. 1905-1915, **$30-35.**

Crocheted purse, black with cut steel beads, c. 1910-1920, **$30-40.**

Sterling silver mesh purse, mount engraved with scrolling foliage, set with blue stones, weighs 6 oz., c. 1910, **$350-360.**

Art Deco silver-mounted evening bag, black satin, lavender lining, silver mount set with green and black onyx and marcasites, 1920-1930, **$130-150.**

Beaded purse, opalescent beads on brown crochet, c. 1920-1930, **$120-125.**

Beaded purse, white, red, and turquoise beads on white, Indian motif, c. 1920-1925, **$60-70.**

Beaded purse, navy silk, hand beaded with carnival glass beads, c. 1920-1930, **$35-40.**

Beaded purse, gold and silver beads, silk lined, c. 1920-1925, **$60-70.**

Beaded purse, brown, red, white paisley design on celluloid frame, c. 1920-1930, **$80-90.**

Hand-embroidered purse in green and yellow, c. 1920-1925, **$40-45.**

Italian evening bag, black antelope with silver mount cast with scrolling foliage, set with amethyst and marcasites, 1920-1930, **$250-275.**

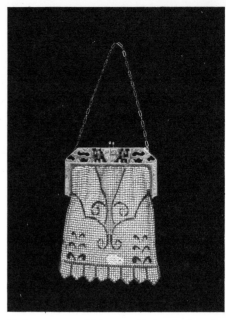

Mesh purse, enameled in green, black and yellow, Art Deco style, c. 1920-1930, **$70-80.**

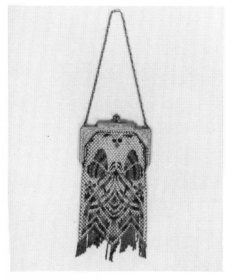

Mesh purse, enameled in pastel on white, gold wash frame, c. 1920-1930, **$60-65.**

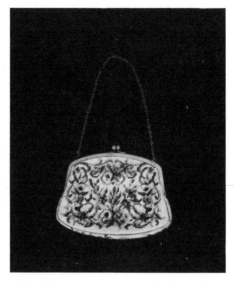

Petit-point purse, pastel floral on white, handmade, c. 1920-1930, **$50-60.**

Chinese silk purse, black, hand-embroidered, c. 1920-1930, **$125-140.**

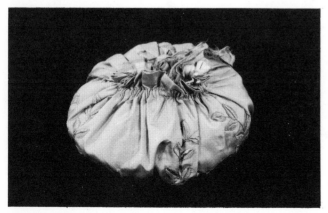

Silk purse, green, drawstring, handmade, hand-embroidered, c. 1920-1930, **$20-25.**

Beaded purse, black velvet and silk, jet beads, c. 1925-1930, **$50-55.**

Beaded purse, black carnival glass beads on ecru crochet, celluloid wrist handles, c. 1925-1930, **$50-60.**

Beaded purse, lime green glass beads on green silk, c. 1925-1930, **$50-60.**

Beaded purse, blue, red, green beads, silk lining, c. 1925-1935, **$80-90.**

Hand-beaded clutch, cut steel beads on black silk, label reads "Made in France," c. 1925-1930, **$35-40.**

Mesh drawstring purse, gold-plated, c. 1925-1930, **$40-45.**

Beaded purse, blue carnival glass and cut steel beads, c. 1925-1930, **$75-80.**

Beaded purse, lime green and gray beads, silk lining, c. 1925-1930, **$75-80.**

53

Hand-tooled leather purse, Art Deco styling, c. 1925-1930, $50-60.

Mesh purse, gold wash, Whiting and Davis, c. 1925-1935, $30-40.

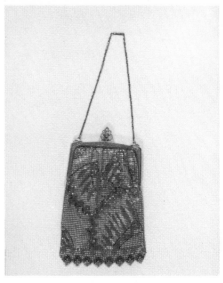

Mesh purse, enameled in bright pastels on gold plate, Whiting and Davis, c. 1925-1935, $90-100.

Mesh purse, enameled in aqua and black on yellow, Art Deco style, Whiting and Davis, c. 1925-1935, $80-90.

Brown alligator purse with feet, c. 1930-1940, $110-120.

Yellow silk beaded purse, hand-beaded design, label reads "Made in France," c. 1930-1935, $45-50.

Beaded purse, white and black beads, c. 1930-1935, $35-40.

Green floral print cloth purse, cotton, velvet buttons, handmade, c. 1930-1935, $10-15.

Brown alligator purse, entire skin, c. 1940-1950, **$110-120.**

Lizard skin purse, gray, c. 1950-1960, **$30-40.**

Lizard skin purse, brown, c. 1950-1960, **$25-30.**

Ladies' Clothing

Blouses and Waists

Victorian and Edwardian blouses or "waists," as they were called back then, are very popular and highly collectible. Lovely elaborate cotton or linen high-neck waists are being reproduced today and can be seen in leading fashion stores. Collectible waists are very valuable if found in excellent condition. Most were lavishly decorated with lace insets, sometimes handmade, or were adorned with delicate hand embroidery.

Vintage blouses from all periods are collectible and very wearable. The wonderful thing about collectible blouses is that they can be worn easily with the styles of today.

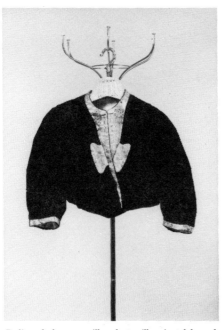

Bodice, dark aqua, silk velvet, silk oriental brocade trim, silk brocade floral lining, lavishly embroidered with piping, c. 1880-1895, **$95-125.**

Waist, ecru handwoven linen with green hand embroidery, c. 1880-1890, **$80-90.**

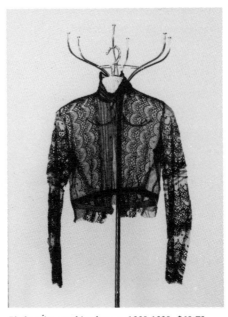

Black waist, machine lace, c. 1880-1890, **$60-70.**

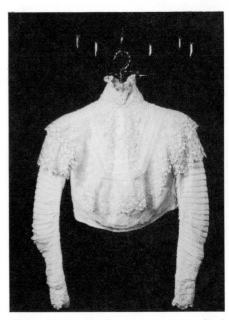

White cotton waist, lace and net, cotton lined, c. 1880-1895, **$150-175.**

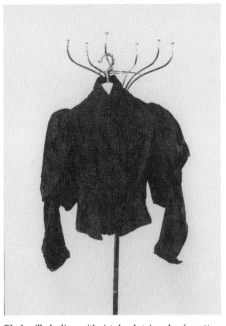

Waist, white cotton net and lace, c. 1880-1900, **$150-175.**

Black silk bodice with jet bead trim, leg-ó-mutton sleeves, hooks in front, c. 1890-1910, **$80-90.**

Silk crepe de chine waist, cutwork, hooks down the side, c. 1890-1900, **$90-100.**

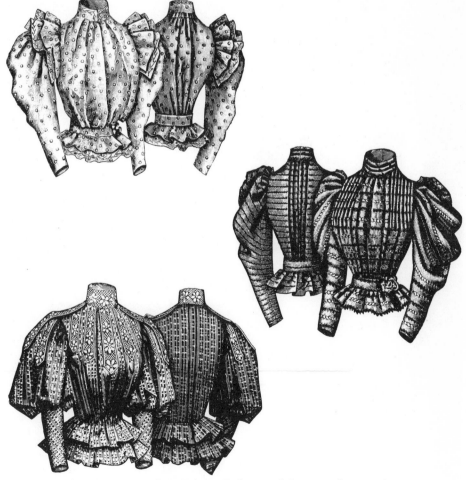

Waist, white silk with black embroidered trim, c. 1890-1900, **$100-110.**

Silk waists, c. 1894, from Victorian Fashions and Costumes, **$70-80 each.**

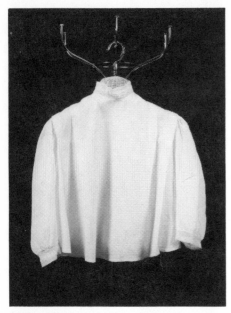

White cotton waist, lace neck, pearl buttons, c. 1895-1910, **$65-75.**

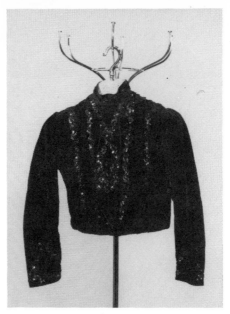

Velvet bodice, wine with black sequin trim, hooks in back, c. 1900-1910, **$70-75.**

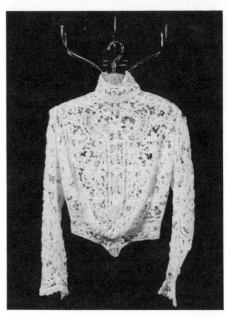

Waist, handmade Battenberg lace, c. 1900-1910, **$200-225.**

Waist, white cotton with lace inset, c. 1900-1910, **$50-60.**

Waist, white cotton net and lace, silk lining, c. 1900-1910, **$80-100.**

White cotton waist, starched collar, c. 1900-1910, **$50-60.**

Waist, white cotton with hand embroidery, c. 1900-1910, **$70-80.**

Ladies' silk waists advertised in the 1902 Sears, Reobuck & Co. Catalogue, **$55-80 each.**

Ladies' sateen and wash waists, from the 1902 Sears, Roebuck & Co. Catalogue, **$40-65 each.**

Ladies' lawn wash waists, from the 1902 Sears, Roebuck & Co. Catalogue, **$80-100 each.**

Waist, white cotton and eyelet, c. 1910-1920, $70-75.

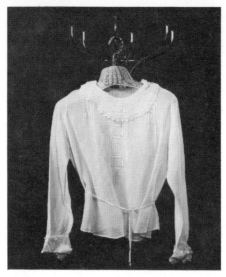

Waist, white cotton with cutwork and embroidery, c. 1910-1920, $50-60.

Waist, white cotton net and lace, c. 1910-1920, $75-100.

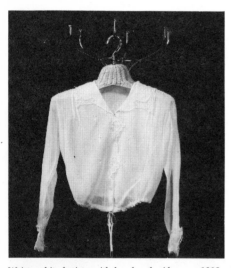

Waist, white batiste with hand embroidery, c. 1910-1920, $50-60.

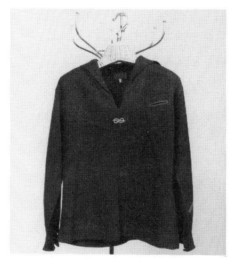

Wool midi, navy, label reads "Robert Evans Marine Togs," c. World War I, $25-30.

Waist, white batiste with lace insert, c. 1910-1920, $50-60.

White cotton waist, c. 1915-1920, $25-30.

Blouse, purple, silk velvet, enameled buttons, never worn, c. 1920-1930, $40-50.

White cotton blouse, embroidered collar, c. 1920-1930, $40-45.

White lined pullover, silk georgette, c. 1920-1930, **$25-30.**

Mint green beaded silk georgette pullover, c. 1920-1930, **$80-90.**

Blouse, ecru lace and hand-embroidered linen insert, velvet trim, c. 1920-1930, **$70-80.**

Silk crepe de chine blouse, lavender, embroidered with piping, c. 1920-1930, **$50-60.**

Blouse, white cotton and eyelet, c. 1920-1930, **$25-30.**

Blouse, ecru silk georgette with multicolored embroidery, c. 1920-1930, **$40-45.**

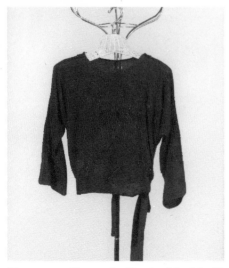

Blouse, navy silk crepe de chine, hand beaded with carnival glass beads, c. 1920-1930, **$70-75.**

Waist, silk pongee with embroidery and tucks, c. 1920-1930, **$40-50.**

Black silk waist, crepe de chine, hand-embroidered flowers, c. 1920-1925, **$45-50.**

61

*Rayon blouse, multicolored floral print, shirred shoulders, c. 1935-1945, **$20-25.***

*Yellow rayon blouse, padded shoulders, button back, c. 1935-1945, **$30-35.***

*Blouse, red rayon with tropical print, label reads "Made in California," c. 1935-1945, **$40-45.***

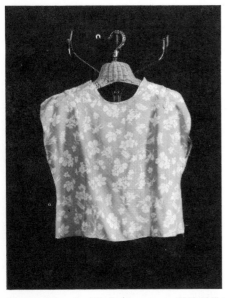

*Blouse, pink and white floral rayon, c. 1940-1945, **$12-15.***

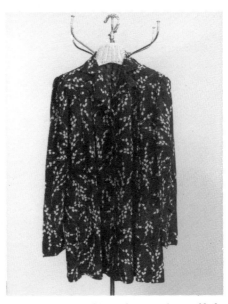

*Maternity blouse, white and gray print on black, c. 1940-1950, **$30-35.***

*Blouse, white nylon lace, button back, c. 1950-1960, **$20-25.***

*White knit pullover, beaded, c. 1950-1960, **$25-30.***

*Blouse, white lace print nylon, button back, c. 1950-1960, **$15-18.***

Dresses

There is tremendous diversity in style and prices for this catagory of vintage clothing. Some dresses made by famous designers of the past are bringing hundreds, even thousands, of dollars. Other less valuable vintage dresses are sought avidly as wearing apparel. As an example, antique car owners often search for clothing to match the period of their cars. Fashion-conscious women buy the lavish silk and crepe dresses of the 1930s and 1940s for day or evening wear.

The best thing about wearing vintage clothing is that you will never see another person wearing the same dress you are!

Day dress, white and pink striped cotton, carved jet buttons, black braid trim, handmade, c. 1860-1865, **$175-200.**

Dress, amethyst and lavender striped two-piece, trimmed with royal purple and black silk fringe, c. 1860-1865, **$140-160.**

Dress, changeable red or green moiré faille, dark green velvet trim, gilt metal and peridot button, c. 1860-1870, **$150-175.**

©Sotheby Parke-Bernet. Agent: Editorial Photocolor Archives.

Opera toilette, c. 1871, from Victorian Fashions and Costumes, **$400-450.**

An evening toilette from Victorian Fashions and Costumes, *c. 1872,* **$700-800.**

Pink silk and yellow chiffon ball gown, requires a bustle, c. 1875-1885, **$275-300.**

Two-piece tea dress, yellow gauze and silk, white lace trim, c. 1880-1890, **$200-250.**

Promenade costume, including parasol and hat, c. 1876, from Victorian Fashions and Costumes, **$600-700.**

A street costume and house gown combination, c. 1889, from Victorian Fashions and Costumes, **$400-450.**

Polonaise costume, c. 1881, from Victorian Fashions and Costumes, **$400-500.**

Outdoor toilettes, c. 1889, from Victorian Fashions and Costumes. Dress on left, **$350-400;** dress on right, **$300-350.**

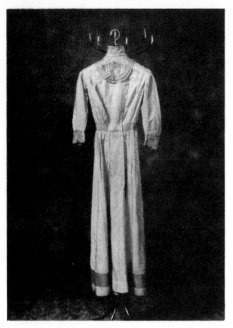

Day dress, silk pongee brocade, lace inset, c. 1890-1900, **$150-160.**

Ball gown, black chiffon over lilac satin, two-piece, label reads "H. Grazer, 106 Main Street, NY," c. 1890-1900, **$150-200.**

Ivory wedding dress, crinkled silk, silk lace, c. 1890-1900, **$275-300.**

Day dress, black print on lavender silk, c. 1890-1900, **$160-175.**

Day dress, green iridescent silk, lace trim, handmade, c. 1890-1900, **$200-225.**

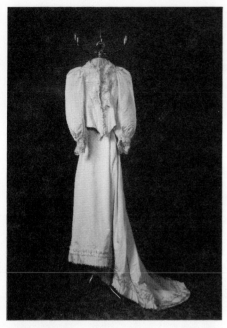

Ivory silk wedding dress, cotton lace, c. 1890-1900, **$250-300.**

Evening dress, royal blue lightweight gabardine, net and silk satin, self-colored piping, white lace, black velvet trim, c. 1890-1900, **$200-225.**

White wedding dress, silk satin, hand-beaded waist band, Battenberg lace-style silk collar, comes with photograph of bride wearing dress, c. 1890-1900, **$300-350.**

An evening gown designed by Worth, c. 1893, from Victorian Fashions and Costumes, **$6,000-7,000.**

Wedding dress and reception dresses, c. 1893, from Victorian Fashions and Costumes. *Wedding dress,* **$300-350;** *reception dresses,* **$150-170 each.**

Commencement gowns, c. 1893 from Victorian Fashions and Costumes, **$300-350 each.**

Summer gown with parasol and hat, c. 1894, from Victorian Fashions and Costumes, **$400-500.**

Paris toilette by Pingat, from Toilettes *magazine, January 1895,* **$175-200.**

Late summer promenade costumes pictured in the September 1895 issue of Toilettes *magazine,* **$250-300 each.**

Bridal costumes shown in the May 1895 issue of Toilette magazine, **$350-400 each.**

Evening dress by Worth, from Toilettes magazine, January 1895, **$4,000-5,000.**

Wedding dress and dress for the mother of the bride, c. 1896, from Victorian Fashions and Costumes. Wedding dress, **$350-375;** mother's dress, **$175-200.**

Paris walking costume with parasol and hat, from Victorian Fashions and Costumes, c. 1896, **$500-575.**

Cashmere gown, c. 1897, from Victorian Fashions and Costumes, **$275-300.**

Cashmere gown with black ruchings, c. 1897, from Victorian Fashions and Costumes, **$175-200.**

Reception gown, c. 1897, from Victorian Fashions and Costumes, **$400-500.**

Day dress, silk pongee, white lace trim, c. 1900-1910, **$85-100.**

Day dress, purple and lavender floral print silk, c. 1900-1910, **$160-170.**

Day dress, gold linen with embroidery, c. 1900-1910, **$180-200.**

Brown corduroy day dress, ecru lace, wooden buttons, peach velvet trim, c. 1900-1910, **$180-200.**

©Sotheby Parke-Bernet. Agent: Editorial Photocolor Archives.

Dress, black lace over oyster silk, three-dimensional floral crochet lace yoke, cuffs and high collar, label reads "L.J. Sexton, Brooklyn, NY," c. 1900-1910, **$150-175.**

Black and white calico cotton day dress, handmade, c. 1900-1910, **$150-175.**

Evening dress, green silk satin with embroidered lamé, c. 1900-1910, **$150-170.**

Black wool jumper, silk trim, c. 1900-1910, **$80-90.**

Evening dress, green silk, white net, floral appliques, white beads, c. 1900-1910, **$160-170.**

Lingerie dress, white gauze, white cotton lace, c. 1900-1910, **$180-200.**

©Sotheby Parke-Bernet. Agent: Editorial Photocolor Archives.

White cotton lingerie dress, bands and squares of lace worked with broderie anglaise and tucks, c. 1900-1910, **$500-550.**

Two-piece lingerie dress, white cotton, lace insets, c. 1900-1910, **$175-200.**

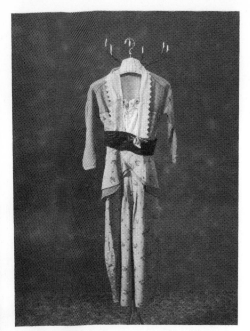

Tea dress, floral print on blue silk, black velvet sash, c. 1900-1910, **$190-200.**

©Sotheby Parke-Bernet. Agent: Editorial Photocolor Archives.

Lingerie dress, white cotton, lace insets, collar trimmed with robin's-egg blue satin and black velvet, c. 1900-1910, **$275-300.**

Tea dress, pink gauze and velvet brocade, lavender velvet sash, c. 1900-1910, **$200-225.**

Wedding dress, white hand-embroidered linen and Battenberg lace insets with train, handmade, c. 1900-1910, **$450-500.**

Cream-colored wedding dress, silk brocade, silk lace, c. 1900-1910, **$150-170.**

White cotton lingerie dress, lace insets, c. 1905-1920, **$120-130.**

Day Dress, white cotton with tucked bodice, c. 1910-1920, **$20-30.**

Day dress, gold print cotton, two-piece, tunic style, c. 1910-1920, **$160-170.**

Day dress, yellow gauze, white lace, black trim, c. 1910-1920, **$75-85.**

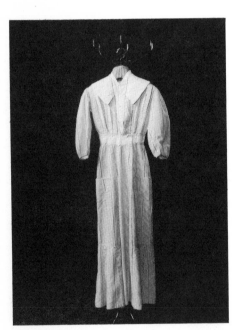

Day dress, black stripe on white cotton, c. 1910-1920, **$60-70.**

Day dress, blue with pastel floral print silk crepe de chine, self-colored velvet ribbon, white lace trim, c. 1910-1920, **$80-90.**

Jumper, white and pink striped cotton, c. 1910-1920, **$55-65.**

Lingerie dress, white dotted swiss, circular cotton lace insets, c. 1910-1920, **$175-200.**

White cotton lace lingerie dress, c. 1910-1920, **$300-400.**

Lingerie dress, white gauze, orange embroidery, c. 1910-1920, **$130-140.**

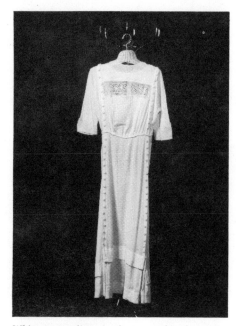

Lingerie dress, white cotton eyelet, c. 1910-1920, **$200-225.**

White gauze lingerie dress, machine-lace trim, c. 1910-1915, **$75-100.**

Lingerie dress, ecru cotton lace, c. 1910-1920, **$140-150.**

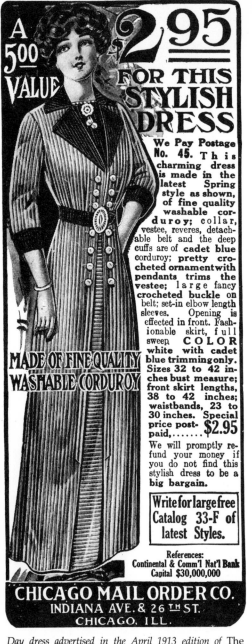

A $5.00 VALUE

2.95 FOR THIS STYLISH DRESS

We Pay Postage No. 45. This charming dress is made in the latest Spring style as shown, of fine quality washable corduroy; collar, vestee, reveres, detachable belt and the deep cuffs are of **cadet blue corduroy;** pretty crocheted ornament with pendants trims the vestee; large fancy crocheted buckle on belt; set-in elbow length sleeves. Opening is effected in front. Fashionable skirt, full sweep. **COLOR** white with cadet blue trimming only. Sizes 32 to 42 inches bust measure; front skirt lengths, 38 to 42 inches; waistbands, 23 to 30 inches. Special price postpaid,....... **$2.95**

We will promptly refund your money if you do not find this stylish dress to be a big bargain.

MADE OF FINE QUALITY WASHABLE CORDUROY

Write for large free Catalog 33-F of latest Styles.

References:
Continental & Comm'l Nat'l Bank
Capital $30,000,000

CHICAGO MAIL ORDER CO.
INDIANA AVE. & 26TH ST.
CHICAGO, ILL.

Day dress advertised in the April 1913 edition of The People's Home Journal, **$85-100.**

FREE Your Copy of America's Best Fashion Guide

AT PHILIPSBORN'S you can buy your Waist, Dress, Suit, Skirt or any kind of Wearing Apparel, at savings so startling that it will be hard to realize how they are possible.

AT PHILIPSBORN'S you are protected against any disappointment by our Guarantee to satisfy you or refund your money.

AT PHILIPSBORN'S you will find the ideal shopping place patronized by over One Million Women who insist upon securing the biggest possible values for every dollar spent.

Here Is A Sensational Value

A65070 — *Richly embroidered, Voile dress. Collar, tie, loops and girdle and rosebud ornaments at bottom of silk messaline. Skirt tunic with plaited flounce. Colors: white with white, gold or light blue messaline trimming. Sizes: Bust 32-44. 36-44 front length. No hem. A $7 value,*
PRICE PREPAID **$4.98.**
A65080 — *Same Style For Small Women or Misses. Sizes: Bust 32-38. Skirt length 36-39. No hem.*
PRICE PREPAID **$4.98.**

Delivery Charges Prepaid Everywhere

Write for Book No. 355

A65070-A65080
THIS $7.00 VOILE DRESS SPECIAL **$4.98** PREPAID

PHILIPSBORN
The Outer Garment House
212-214 W. ADAMS ST. CHICAGO.

Advertisement for voile dress from the April 1913 People's Home Journal, **$200-225.**

Lingerie dress, white cotton with lace insets and tucks, c. 1913, People's Home Journal, **$250-300.**

Dress advertised in the April 1913 People's Home Journal, **$200-250**

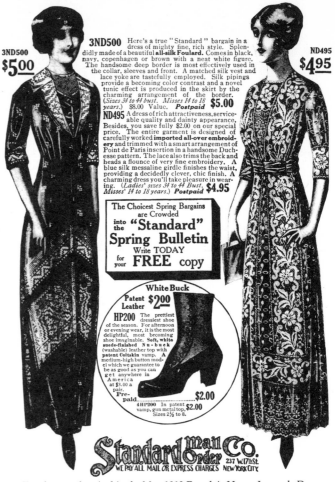

Advertisement from the April 1913 edition of The People's Home Journal. *Dress on left,* **$225-250;** *dress on right,* **$100-125.**

Two dresses advertised in the May 1913 People's Home Journal. *Dress on left,* **$80-90;** *dress on right,* **$200-225.**

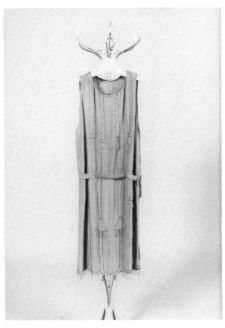

©Sotheby Parke-Bernet. Agent: Editorial Photocolor Archives.

Tea dress, yellow batiste, white lace insets, c. 1915-1925, **$225-250.**

Black silk beaded dress with red and gray beads, label reads "Made in France," c. 1918-1920, **$400-500.**

Beaded dress, green silk crepe de chine, hand beaded, c. 1920-1930, **$140-150.**

Beaded dress, brown georgette, hand beaded, c. 1920-1930, **$120-130.**

Beaded dress, net sewn overall with yellow and crystal beads, peplum and hem worked with gold sequins and bugle beads, c. 1920-1930, **$250-275.**

Beaded dress, black silk net on silk satin, aqua and lamé sash hand beaded with jet beads and lozenges, c. 1920-1930, **$150-180.**

Beaded dress, black beads on chiffon, rhinestone buckle, c. 1920-1930, **$180-200.**

Beaded dress, black beads and sequins completely cover net in Art Deco designs, c. 1920-1930, **$400-500.**

Bright pink satin costume, yellow gauze, gold lamé and black velvet, c. 1920-1930, **$50-60.**

Black net evening dress, gold lamé, c. 1920-1930, **$225-250.**

Beaded dress, ivory satin and chiffon, flowers, leaves and scrolls worked in pewter, crystal beads, c. 1920-1930, **$200-250.**

Evening dress, black silk satin and net, hand-beaded sash, dropped waist, full length, c. 1920-1930, **$125-130.**

Day dress, white cotton, hand-embroidered batiste insert, c. 1920-1925, **$90-100.**

Beaded dress, black chiffon embroidered with crystal beads and pastes, c. 1920-1930, **$300-350.**

Tea dress, cream georgette, hand-smocked and pleated, c. 1920-1930, **$140-150.**

Ecru lace tea dress, peach silk lining (restored), c. 1920-1930, **$50-60.**

Beaded dress, teal blue silk, hand beaded, c. 1925-1930, **$150-170.**

Beaded dress, gold silk satin, tunic style, hand beaded, c. 1925-1930, **$150-160.**

Brown velvet beaded dress, orange beadwork and embroidery, full length, label reads "Made in Paris," c. 1925-1930, **$160-175.**

Day dress, orange floral print on yellow batiste, c. 1925-1935, **$50-60.**

Day dress, black and pink floral print on white silk, c. 1925-1930, **$40-50.**

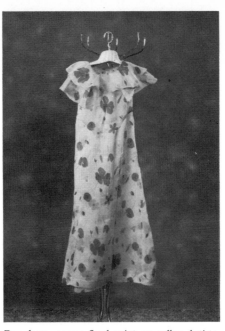

Day dress, navy and white rayon, c. 1925-1935, **$45-60.**

Day dress, orange floral print on yellow batiste, c. 1925-1935, **$50-60.**

Day dress, navy and beige georgette, rust and beige machine embroidery, c. 1925-1930, **$60-70.**

Evening dress, gold lamé on pink silk, pastel floral appliques, c. 1925-1930, **$150-160.**

Evening dress, brown and beige chiffon, velvet and rhinestone appliques, matching scarf, c. 1925-1930, **$80-90.**

Evening dress with jacket, green silk satin and ecru lace, c. 1925-1930, **$80-90.**

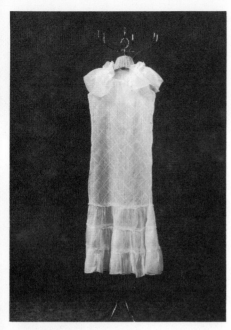

Graduation dress, white batiste, cross-stitched, c. 1925-1930, **$50-60.**

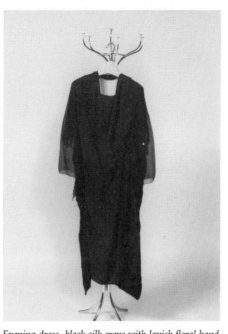

Evening dress, black silk crepe with lavish floral hand embroidery all over shawl back, chiffon sleeves, c. 1925-1930, **$75-100.**

Wedding dress, white chiffon and silk, hand-beaded, c. 1925-1930, **$125-140.**

Day dress, white rayon crepe with pastel floral hand embroidery, c. 1930-1940, **$50-60.**

Ecru silk crepe de chine day dress, brown piped embroidery, c. 1930-1935, **$35-45.**

Green moiré day dress, ecru lace collar, c. 1930-1940, **$50-55.**

Day dress, orange and red print on ecru silk, c. 1930-1935, **$70-80.**

Designer dress by Fortuny. Ruby velvet stenciled in gilt with a wide band of Islamic motifs down front, back and sleeves, label reads "Mariano Fortuny — Venise," c. 1930-1940, **$1,300-1,400.**

Designer dress and cape by Fortuny. Dress is made of butterscotch pleated silk satin, edged with Venetian amber glass beads, striped in red and brown, c. 1930-1940, **$1,500-2,000.** The cape is made of butterscotch gauze stenciled with trees and bands of scrolling foliage, edged with Venetian amber glass beads striped in red and brown. Label reads "Fabrique en Italie — Fortuny Depose — Made in Italy," **$800-1,200.**

Designer dress by Vionnet. Black panne velvet, self slip, label reads "Madeline Vionnet," c. 1930-1940, **$7,300-7,500.**

Evening dress, aqua and black silk velvet, c. 1930-1940, **$130-140.**

Black chiffon evening dress, white cotton lace, c. 1930-1935, **$80-90.**

Evening dress, burgundy silk velvet, c. 1930-1935, **$60-80.**

Evening dress, brown silk satin, chiffon, and velvet brocade, three-piece, c. 1930-1935, **$100-120.**

Evening dress, pink floral print on black chiffon, c. 1930-1940, **$70-80.**

Prom dress, aqua chiffon, black and white print, black velvet ribbon, bias cut, c. 1930-1940, **$50-60.**

Tea dress, pink eyelet, rayon satin lining, blue silk sash and flower, c. 1930-1935, **$80-90.**

Tea dress, white dotted swiss, bias cut, c. 1930-1935, **$65-80.**

Wedding dress, white chiffon with satin appliques, c. 1930-1940, **$80-90.**

Day dress, brown and white rayon, ecru cotton, machine-embroidered collar, c. 1935-1940, **$40-50.**

Day dress, black and white print on chartreuse rayon crepe, black suede trim, c. 1935-1940, **$70-80.**

Day dress, pink rayon, blue piping, padded shoulders, c. 1935-1945, **$25-35.**

Designer dress by Alix. Ivory matte silk jersey, self slip, label reads "Alix," c. 1935-1940, **$500-550.**

Blue taffeta evening dress, white lace sleeves, side zipper, c. 1935-1940, **$50-60.**

Evening dress, black rayon crepe, rhinestone trim, high padded shoulders, c. 1935-1945, **$90-100.**

Prom dress, two-piece black net with machine-embroidered daisies, c. 1935-1940, **$60-70.**

White satin wedding dress, 1935-1940, **$80-90.**

Designer dress by Lanvin. Black taffeta sewn overall with four triangle pinwheels of layered inverted sequins, label reads "Jeanne Lanvin — Paris — Hiver, 1938 — 1939 — Unis — France," **$400-500.**

Designer dress by Lanvin. Raspberry and cerise chiffon, self slip and belt, label reads "Jeanne Lanvin — Unis — France — 15 — 7, 1939," **$700-800.**

Evening dress, rust silk velvet, gold sequin trim, c. 1940-1945, **$75-85.**

Evening dress, gray machine-embroidered chiffon, gray satin slip, blue and purple chiffon and silk sash, c. 1940-1945, **$85-95.**

Evening dress, green rayon crepe, lace and beaded collar, padded shoulders, c. 1940-1945, **$70-75.**

Evening dress, black knit studded with rhinestones, c. 1940-1950, **$45-50.**

Evening dress, pink chiffon, silver beadwork, c. 1940-1950, **$80-90.**

Wedding dress, white satin and chiffon, c. 1940-1945, **$60-75.**

Day dress, pink print on cotton, wrap style, c. 1945-1950, **$15-20.**

Evening dress, black iridescent sequins, black net skirt, c. 1945-1950, **$90-100.**

Evening dress, white lace appliques and rhinestones on pink cotton and rayon blend, c. 1950-1960, **$50-60.**

Designer dress by Balenciaga. Black velvet embroidered openwork leaves, pale beige mesh spaghetti straps, label reads "Balenciaga — 10, Avenue Georges V, Paris," c. 1950-1960, **$2,800-3,000.**

Prom dress, lavender net over satin, c. 1950-1960, **$50-60.**

Prom dress, yellow net and lace, lavender plastic floral trim, c. 1950-1960, **$60-65.**

Prom dress, white net and acetate, c. 1950-1960, **$40-50.**

White nylon prom dress, satin lining, gold embroidery, c. 1950-1960, **$25-35.**

Wedding dress, white cotton lace, c. 1950-1955, **$50-60.**

Green knit day dress, green beadwork, label reads "Vogue Couterier Design," c. 1955-1960, **$70-80.**

Designer dress by Sachs. Champagne rayon knit, gold rhinestones in silver metal ornament, label reads "Paul Sachs Original," never worn, c. 1955, **$250-350.**

Green chiffon evening dress, label reads "Harold Sheer, Beverly Hills," c. 1955-1960, **$125-150.**

Evening dress, brown rayon crepe, sequins on collar, label reads "Harold Sheer, Beverly Hills," c. 1955-1960, **$100-125.**

Pink nylon evening dress, c. 1955-1960, **$20-25.**

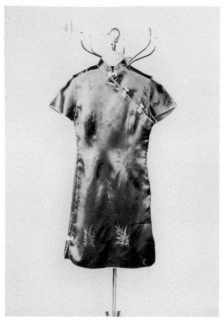

Oriental dress, red silk brocade, c. 1960, **$40-45.**

Lingerie

"They don't make them like they used to" is an accurate statement when referring to vintage lingerie. The earliest lingerie was mostly all-white cotton or linen lavishly trimmed with laces and eyelets. Most were made to be durable, so they could be washed and starched over and over again. Because of this durability, many of the earliest pieces are still found in excellent condition. Contemporary women are buying vintage lingerie of this sort for wearing apparel. Lacy camisoles and petticoats are often worn together as a light summer outfit. Nightgowns with hand-crocheted yokes look lovely when belted and worn as summer dresses.

Robe (possibly Chinese), handmade, brown silk with brown and red silk hand-embroidery, hand-quilted, c. 1875-1895, **$250-300.**

Lingerie and nightwear, c. 1876, from Victorian Fashions and Costumes. *Left to right: night sacque,* **$100-110;** *batiste nightcap,* **$20-30;** *muslin petticoat,* **$75-100;** *night dress,* **$125-150.**

White linen camisole, handmade, c. 1880-1890, **$75-85.**

Petticoat, white cotton, handmade, cutwork, tucks, eyelet, minor damage, c. 1880-1895, **$80-90.**

Petticoat, white cotton, eyelet trim, broderie anglaise inset, button waist, c. 1880-1895, **$120-130.**

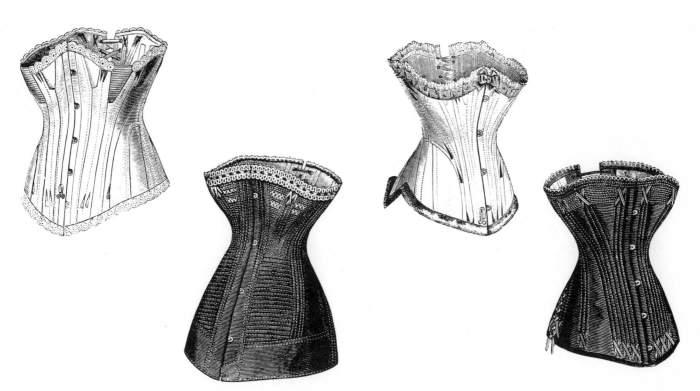

Corsets, c. 1882, from Victorian Fashions and Costumes, **$45-60.**

Hoop slip, white cotton, hooks in back, c. 1885-1895, **$40-50.**

Petticoat, white cotton with train, lace and ribbon trim, c. 1890-1900, **$110-120.**

Linen lawn morning gown (back view) c. 1882, from Victorian Fashions and Costumes, **$200-250.**

Breakfast jacket, c. 1888, from Victorian Fashions and Costumes, **$100-120.**

Dressing gown, cream silk crepe de chine, c. 1890, $175-200.

Petticoat, black polished cotton, ruffles and tucks, c. 1890-1900, $50-55.

Petticoat, white cotton pique, silk satin, dust ruffle, hooks on side, c. 1890-1900, $40-45.

Corsets, c. 1893, from Victorian Fashions and Costumes, **$35-80 each.**

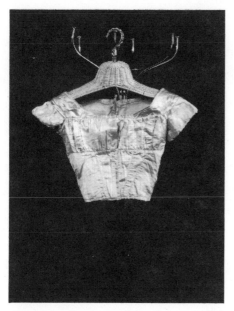

Corset, beige silk satin, boned, laces in front and back, c. 1895-1900, $35-45.

Pantaloons, ecru cotton, handmade, hand-crocheted lace trim, buttonholes for camisole, c. 1895-1895, $30-35.

Corset cover and skirt, c. 1896, from Victorian Fashions and Costumes, **$150-160 set.**

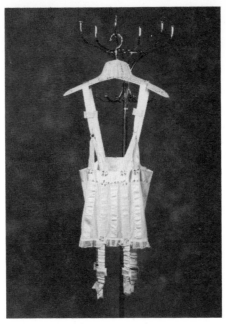

Ivory garter belt, silk and net, floral appliques, rare, c. 1900, **$80-100.**

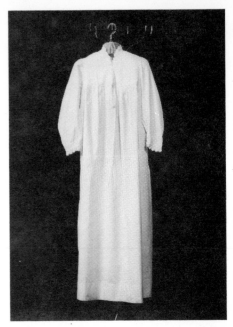

Nightgown, white cotton, eyelet yoke, long sleeves, c. 1900, **$60-65.**

Nightgown, white cotton, eyelet and tuck trim, c. 1900-1915, **$55-80.**

Petticoat, black polished cotton, shirring, rickrack trim, c. 1900-1910, **$40-50.**

Petticoat, white cotton, handmade, hand-crocheted lace inset and trim, tucks, c. 1900-1905, **$125-130.**

Pettipants, white cotton, eyelet trim, side button, c. 1900-1910, **$40-45.**

Nightgown, white cotton, knee length, tucked bib front, lace insets, c. 1905, **$55-65.**

Pantaloons, white cotton, side button, eyelet trim, c. 1905-1910, **$45-50.**

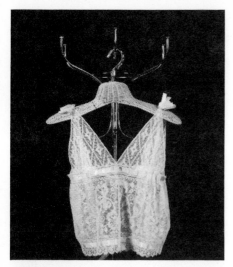

*Camisole, white cotton lace, silk ribbons, c. 1910-1920, **$60-70.***

*White cotton camisole, hand-crocheted yoke, button front, c. 1910-1920, **$35-40.***

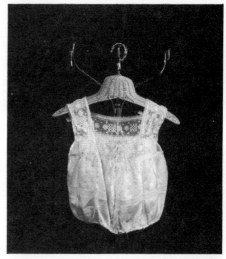

*Camisole, pink silk crepe de chine, lace yoke and inset, button front, c. 1910-1920, **$40-45.***

*White cotton camisole, handmade, hand-crocheted rose yoke, c. 1910-1920, **$40-50.***

*White cotton camisole, handmade, hand crocheted, c. 1910-1915, **$45-50.***

*Pantaloons, split, white cotton, eyelet ruffle, never worn, c. 1910-1915, **$35-40.***

*Split pantaloons, white cotton, tucks and lace trim, c. 1910, **$40-45.***

*Bust confiner, white cotton, eyelet trim, never worn, c. 1915, **$20-25.***

*White linen camisole, lace inset, hooks in back, c. 1915-1925, **$35-45.***

Nightgown, white cotton, hand-crocheted yoke, c. 1915-1925, **$50-55.**

Nightgown, white cotton, hand-crocheted lace around neckline and sleeves, large size, c. 1915-1920, **$35-45.**

Robe, white, pink, and red print cotton, c. 1915-1925, **$35-40.**

Camisole, pink silk satin, hooks in front, c. 1920-1925, **$25-35.**

White cotton camisole, handmade, hand-beaded design, c. 1920-1925, **$35-40.**

Camisole, pink silk, batiste embroidered yoke, never worn, c. 1920, **$40-50.**

Nightgown, peach silk satin, pastel embroidered ecru lace, label reads "Sally Francis," c. 1920-1930, **$30-40.**

Slip, white cotton, drawstring top, mid-calf length, c. 1920-1925, **$35-40.**

Slip, mint green silk crepe de chine, flapper style, c. 1920-1930, **$15-20.**

Step-ins, white cotton, lace trim, c. 1920-1930, **$14-18.**

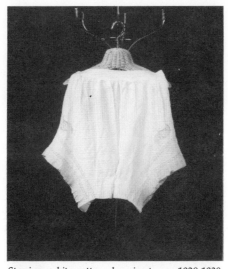

Step-ins, white cotton, lace insets, c. 1920-1930, **$15-20.**

White cotton teddy, cutwork, Irish lace inset, tatted trim, silk straps, c. 1920-1930, **$45-55.**

Pink silk teddy, ecru lace, c. 1920-1930, **$30-35.**

Chemise, black georgette and lace, pink silk flower, c. 1925-1930, **$30-40.**

Kimono, reversible, black and blue floral crepe de chine, knee length, c. 1925-1935, **$50-70.**

Step-ins, pink georgette, elastic waist, c. 1925-1930, **$15-20.**

Nightgown, blue satin, bias cut, lace trim, c. 1940-1945, **$20-30.**

Nightgown, matching bed jacket, pink and pastel floral cotton, bias cut, c. 1940-1945, **$35-40.**

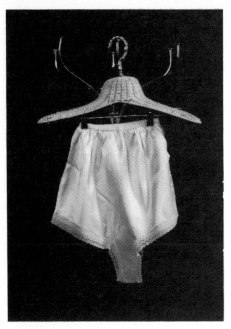

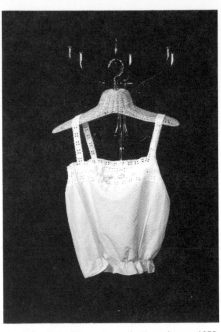

Tap panties, peach rayon satin, never worn, c. 1940-1945, **$10-15.**

Nightgown, peach rayon, lace trim, shirring, bias cut, c. 1945, **$25-35.**

Camisole, light blue cotton, elastic waist, c. 1950-1960, **$15-20.**

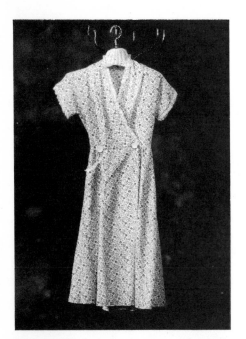

Robe, pastel floral print cotton, wraparound, c. 1950-1955, **$20-25.**

Slip, white net, elastic waist, c. 1955-1960, **$15-20.**

Slip, green and white acetate and net, side zipper, c. 1955-1960, **$20-25.**

Outerwear

The most popular apparel in outerwear collectibles are the beaded sweater of the 1950s and 1960s and the tailored blazer of the late 1930s and early 1940s. Gabardine, which is known for its durability and eye appeal, was a popular fabric for these quality blazers. Seams were sewn to perfection and the jackets were tailored to fit. The quality that was commonplace then is rare today.

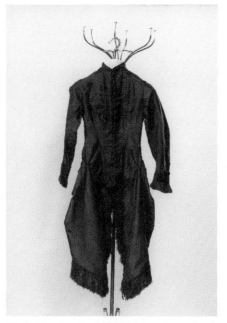

Black silk satin paletot, black silk brocade, crocheted buttons, c. 1870-1885, **$90-100.**

Cape, black silk and lace, silk lined, label reads "B. Altman," c. 1875-1895, **$150-170.**

Cashmere paletots, front and back, c. 1871, from Victorian Fashions and Costumes, **$90-110 each.**

Ladies' ulsters with hoods, c. 1876, from Victorian Fashions and Costumes, **$80-90.**

Cape, black lace with heavy jet-beaded applique, label reads "Mantles and Costumes, Forrett and Loni, Ltd., Dublin and Cork," c. 1880-1895, **$160-180.**

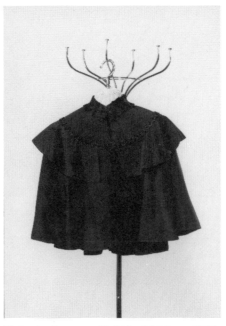

Black gabardine cape with jet-beaded trim, c. 1880-1900, **$80-100.**

Dress coat, black wool, floral silk lining, c. 1880-1890, **$150-175.**

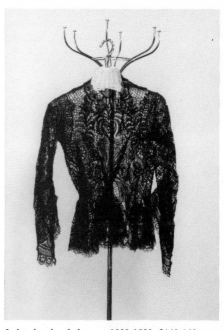

Dress coat, navy wool, black silk trim, c. 1880-1890, **$80-90.**

Dress coat, white wool, moiré collar and cuffs, c. 1880-1900, **$60-75.**

Jacket, handmade lace, c. 1880-1890, **$140-160.**

Jacket, gray silk with lace collar and cuffs, c. 1880-1890, **$50-60.**

Black mourning coat, waterproofed satin, silk tassles, c. 1880-1890, **$75-85.**

Above:
Lace and jet pelerine, c. 1881, from Victorian Fashions and Costumes, **$100-120.**

Above right:
Opera cloaks, c. 1882, from Victorian Fashions and Costumes, **$110-125 each.**

Below right:
Winter wrappings, c. 1884, from Victorian Fashions and Costumes, **$175-200 each.**

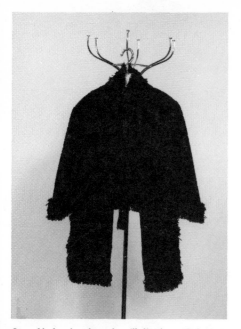

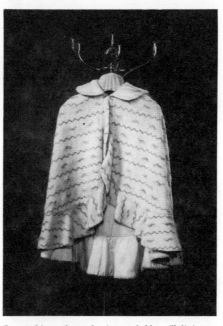

Cape, black velvet brocade, silk lined, c. 1890-1910, **$120-130.**

Cape, white and pastel print wool, blue silk lining, c. 1890-1900, **$70-80.**

Black cotton jacket, leg-o-mutton sleeves, c. 1890-1900, **$50-60.**

Bishop's mantel, c. 1891, from Victorian Fashions and Costumes, **$175-200.**

Dust cloaks by Worth, c. 1892, from Victorian Fashions and Costumes, **$500-600 each.**

Parisian cape with black marten fur border, c. 1893, from Victorian Fashions and Costumes, **$130-150.**

Another cloak by Worth, c. 1893, from Victorian Fashions and Costumes, **$800-900.**

Evening and carriage cloaks by Worth, c. 1894, from Victorian Fashions and Costumes, **$900-1,200.**

A traveling cloak, c. 1894, from Victorian Fashions and Costumes, **$250-300.**

Cape, black plush with monkey fur trim, c. 1895-1905, **$110-125.**

Lady's jacket advertised in the January 1895 issue of Toilettes Magazine, **$80-90.**

Fashion capes, c. 1896, from Victorian Fashions and Costumes, **$140-150 each.**

Black gabardine bolero with hand embroidery, c. 1900-1910, **$45-55.**

Jacket, brown and white calico print cotton, handmade with pearl buttons, c. 1900-1910, **$40-45.**

Navy wool jacket, white wool trim, silk lined, c. 1900-1910, **$45-50.**

Ladies' jackets available from Sears, Roebuck, c. 1902, **$30-60 each.**

Plush capes available from Sears, Roebuck, c. 1902, **$110-150 each.**

Spring and summer capes advertised in the 1902 Sears, Roebuck & Co. Catalogue, **$90-120 each.**

Duster, ecru linen, handmade with hand-embroidery, c. 1910-1920, **$150-175.**

Riding jacket, khaki tweed and trim, c. 1910-1920, **$50-60.**

Gray wool tweed jacket, c. 1910-1920, **$40-50.**

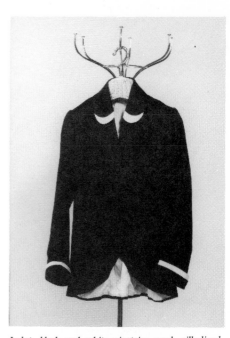

Jacket, black and white pinstripe wool, silk lined, c. 1910-1920, **$50-55.**

Ladies' fur collarettes advertised in the 1902 Sears, Roebuck & Co. Catalogue, **$60-75 each.**

Opera cape, black gabardine hand-embroidered in pastel colors, silk lined, c. 1920-1930, **$250-300.**

Opera cape, pink silk satin brocade woven with gold metallic threads, brown silk velvet, c. 1920-1930, **$160-170.**

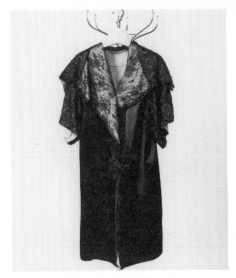

Opera cape, black silk satin with silk lace overlay, c. 1920-1930, **$110-125.**

Opera cape, black silk metallic brocade with red floral print, red velvet collar, reversible, c. 1920-1930, **$175-200.**

Cashmere dress coat, silk lined, c. 1920-1930, **$80-100.**

Dress coat, black silk embroidered brocade, brown muskrat trim, c. 1920-1930, **$70-80.**

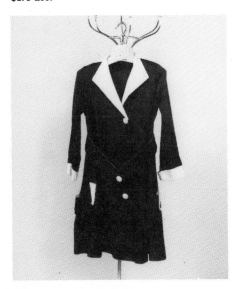

Duster, black and white linen, c. 1920-1930, **$50-60.**

Jacket, ivory hand-embroidered silk, c. 1920-1930, **$125-150.**

Evening coat, black silk brocade, hand-beaded, Norwegian fox collar, c. 1925-1930, **$175-200.**

Cape, pink silk crepe, label reads "Jean Patou, 7 Rue St. Florentin, Paris, 92888," c. 1925-1932, **$275-300.**

Jacket, teal blue chiffon with gold sequins, c. 1925-1935, **$75-80.**

White lace jacket, c. 1925-1930, **$40-50.**

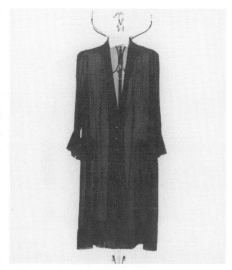

Tunic, black silk georgette, shirred shoulders, pleated trim, c. 1925-1930, **$45-50.**

Tunic, beige raw silk with black moiré trim, c. 1925-1930, **$40-50.**

Black net bolero with gold sequins, c. 1930-1940, **$30-35.**

Kimono, multicolored silk, lined, c. 1930-1940, **$50-60.**

Sweater shawl, lavender, hand knit, c. 1930-1940, **$15-20.**

Costume capelet, pink moiré taffeta, c. 1935-1940, **$25-30.**

111

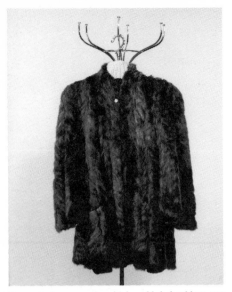

Fur coat, brown ermine, high padded shoulders, can be unsnapped and made into a cape, c. 1935-1945, **$275-300.**

Jacket, ecru gabardine, satin lined, high padded shoulders, label reads "Custom Tailored," c. 1935-1945, **$70-80.**

Dress coat, gray gabardine, high padded shoulders, c. 1940-1945, **$35-40.**

Silver fox jacket, spiraling pieced sleeves, bands of black satin between the pelts and along the undersides of the sleeves, c. 1940-1950, **$800-900.**

Fur jacket, brown fox, label reads "Henry Marshall, Brooklyn," c. 1940-1950, **$250-275.**

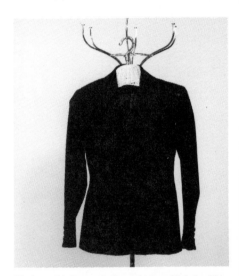

Black wool jacket, satin lined, high padded shoulders, c. 1940-1945, **$45-55.**

Blue wool jacket, neatly tailored, padded shoulders, c. 1940-1945, **$35-40.**

Brown gabardine jacket, self-embroidered trim, satin lining, padded shoulders, c. 1940-1945, **$45-50.**

Sweater, black knit, ostrich feathers, c. 1940-1950, **$50-55.**

112

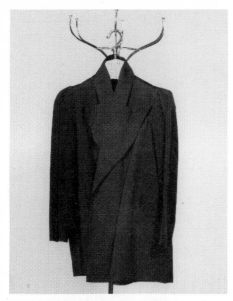

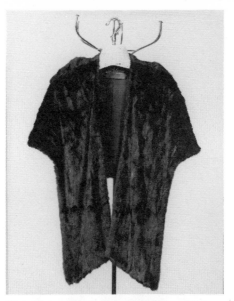

Coat, black taffeta, hip length, c. 1950-1960, **$25-30.**

Fur stole, muskrat, label reads "J.W. Robinson, California," c. 1950-1960, **$110-125.**

Autumn Haze mink coat, label reads "Martha Weathered," c. 1950-1960, **$900-1,100.**

Cashmere sweater, beige, heavy sequin design, lined, c. 1955-1965, **$70-80.**

Beige cashmere sweater, copper colored beads, lined, c. 1955-1965, **$45-60.**

Jacket, blue felt embroidered and appliqued, label reads "Hecho in Mexico," c. 1960-1965, **$25-30.**

Orlon sweater, beige with rust colored beads, lined, c. 1960-1970, **$40-45.**

Sweater, white cashmere, beaded, lined, c. 1960-1970, **$50-75.**

Black cashmere sweater with fox collar, c. 1960-1970, **$80-100.**

White orlon sweater, rabbit collar, c. 1960-1970, **$60-75.**

Sweater, pastel floral embroidery and beads on cream knit, c. 1960-1965, **$35-50.**

Mink coat and hat, black mink pieced horizontally, notched collar, label reads "Alfred Rainer, New York," contemporary, **$1,200-1,600.**

Mink coat, black/brown fur, contemporary, **$800-1,000.**

Norwegian blue fox fur coat, wide vertical pelts, notched lapels, contemporary, **$2,300-2,500.**

Russian sable coat, ankle length, pieced horizontally, wide notched lapel collar, detachable hem made of sable tails, label reads "Henri Bendel, New York," contemporary, **$8,000-10,000.**

Sportswear

From the late 1800s (when women started taking up sports such as golfing or bicycling) to the present time, sportswear has been an important part of every active woman's wardrobe. The most popular apparel for collecting today are the early bicycling outfits, which generally consisted of bloomers, a loose jacket and hat. Split skirts were also worn.

Nostalgic sportswear can be fun to collect and wear.

Ladies' skating suits, c. 1876, from Victorian Fashions and Costumes, **$200-225 each.**

Tennis costume, c. 1881, from Victorian Fashions and Costumes, **$200-225.**

Lady's riding suit, c. 1876, from Victorian Fashions and Costumes, **$140-160.**

Lady's hunting costume, c. 1893, from Victorian Fashions and Costumes, **$125-150.**

Tennis gown, c. 1893, from Victorian Fashions and Costumes, **$175-225.**

Bicycle dress, c. 1894, from Victorian Fashions and Costumes, **$100-140.**

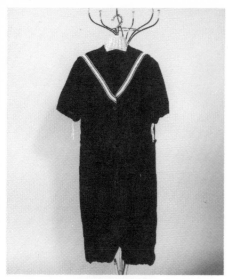

Bloomers, black cotton, c. 1900-1920, **$40-60.**

Riding skirt, khaki cotton, c. 1900-1910, **$35-40.**

Riding skirt, brown corduroy, c. 1900-1910, **$40-50.**

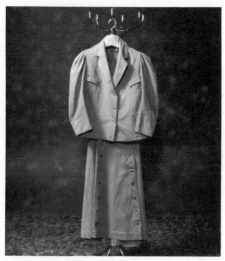

Riding suit, khaki gabardine, c. 1900-1910, **$150-160.**

Tennis skirt, white linen, c. 1900-1910, **$50-60.**

Tennis skirt, white linen, c. 1900-1910, **$70-75.**

Golfing suit, white linen with floral print, c. 1900-1910, **$125-150.**

Golfing suit, white linen with floral print, c. 1900-1910, **$125-135.**

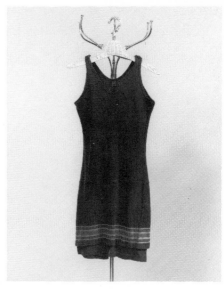

Swimsuit, green wool with flesh-colored stripes, never worn, c. 1910-1920, **$45-55.**

Gym bloomers, black, polished cotton, c. 1910-1920, **$40-50.**

Bloomers, blue and white striped cotton, c. 1910-1920, **$25-35.**

Bloomers, blue cotton, c. 1920-1930, **$35-40.**

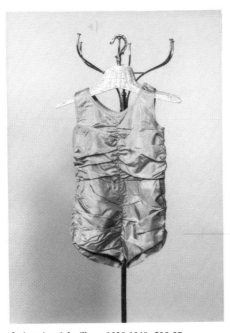

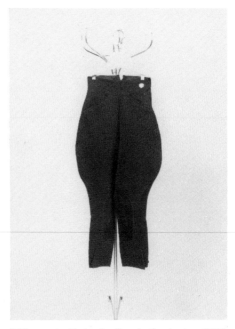

Swimsuit, pink silk, c. 1930-1940, **$30-35.**

Riding pants, black gabardine, leather inset, c. 1940-1945, **$40-45.**

Suits

Women's suits have been popular for years. Since the beginning of the women's rights movement, some say they look more and more like men's suits. The stylish suits of the late 1930s and early 1940s are popular wearing apparel today. The high-padded shoulders, sleek tailored waistlines, and narrow skirts provide a shapely, chic look for today's professional woman.

Above:
Polonaise walking suit, front and back, c. 1873, from Victorian Fashions and Costumes, **$250-275.**

Above right:
Walking suit, c. 1872, from Victorian Fashions and Costumes, **$400-450.**

Below right:
Visiting toilette, c. 1873, from Victorian Fashions and Costumes, **$500-600.**

Ladies' riding suits, c. 1873, from Victorian Fashions and Costumes, **$200-225 each.**

Winter Costume, c. 1875, from Victorian Fashions and Costumes, **$500-550.**

Polonaise walking suit, front and back, c. 1876, from Victorian Fashions and Costumes, **$300-325.**

Dress suit, black silk with white trim and embroidery, c. 1880-1890, **$110-120.**

Riding suit, khaki cotton, wool blend, c. 1880-1890, **$100-120.**

Walking suit, black taffeta, c. 1880-1895, **$140-160.**

Wool walking suit, black and green stripe, c. 1880-1890, **$175-200.**

Black wool mourning suit, c. 1885-1900, **$120-140.**

Walking suit, green tweed, c. 1885-1900, **$150-175.**

Spring walking suits, c. 1885, from Victorian Fashions and Costumes, **$350-385 each.**

Tailor-made suits pictured in the May 1895 issue of Toilettes *magazine,* **$170-190 each.**

Day suit, white seersucker, lace trim, c. 1900-1910, **$150-170.**

Walking suit, gray and black corduroy, white lace trim, c. 1900-1910, **$140-160.**

Walking suit, black and white wool knit, c. 1900-1910, **$130-150.**

Black silk velvet evening suit, white silk lining, c. 1920-1930, **$80-100.**

Dress suit, purple silk, c. 1930-1935, **$60-70.**

Red silk dress suit, c. 1930-1935, **$50-60.**

Dress suit, white and black print rayon, padded shoulders, peplum, c. 1935-1940, **$55-65.**

Dress suit, lavender gabardine, padded shoulders, c. 1935-1942, **$70-75.**

Dress suit, navy gabardine, padded shoulders, c. 1935-1945, **$60-70.**

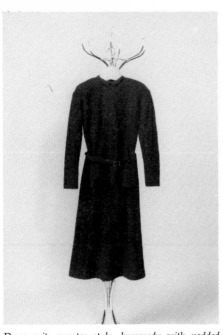

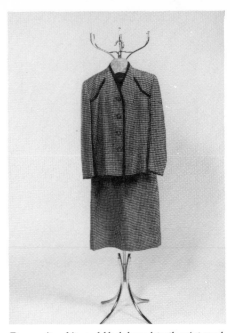

Dress suit, sweater style, burgundy with padded shoulders, c. 1938-1945, **$40-55.**

Dress suit, navy silk, shirred shoulders, c. 1940-1945, **$45-55.**

Dress suit, white and black houndstooth print wool, padded shoulders, c. 1940-1945, **$50-60.**

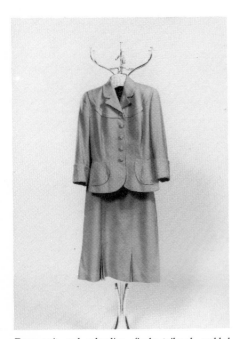

Dress suit, red gabardine, finely tailored, padded shoulders, c. 1940-1945, **$50-60.**

Lounging pantsuit, red and white polka-dot rayon, high padded shoulders, c. 1940-1945, **$50-60.**

Western style suit, rust gabardine with white kid-leather trim, c. 1940-1950, **$60-75.**

Designer suits by Adrian. Left: charcoal wool, velvet trim, label reads "Adrian Original," c. 1945-1950, **$200-250.** *Center: black wool, Roman coin buttons, label reads "Adrian Original," c. 1945,* **$200-250.** *Right: wool, black and white houndstooth overlaid with burgundy windowpane plaid, label reads "Adrian Original," c. 1945,* **$250-260.**

Three-piece dress suit, raw silk and floral rayon, c. 1945-1950, **$40-50.**

Designer suits by Christian Dior. Left: black lightweight wool, label reads "Christian Dior — Paris — Printemps — Ete — 1953, Made in France — 33412," c. 1953, **$100-140.** *Right: black wool, label reads "Christian Dior — Paris Automne — Hiver 1956 — 33244," c. 1956,* **$250-275.**

Designer suits by Chanel. Left: wool, woven in a large houndstooth of black, white and aqua. Cuffs and skirt waistband are aqua, pink and gold striped lamé, lion's head gilt and enamel buttons, c. 1955-1965, **$250-275.** *Center: nubby pale pink tweed, pockets and cuffs trimmed with pale pink silk linen piping, gilt lion's head buttons, label reads "Chanel — 25130,"* **$175-190.** *Right: diagonal stripes of black and white tweed, trimmed with black knitted bands, label reads "Chanel — Made in France — 68432,"* **$225-250.**

Designer suits by Balenciaga. Left: three-piece, rust and green plaid on cream, wooden buttons, label reads "Balenciaga — 10 Avenue George V Paris — 97691," c. 1960-1965, **$60-75.** *Right: three-piece, gray and white checked wool, label reads "Balenciaga — 10 Avenue George V Paris — 71709," c. 1960-1965,* **$80-100.**

Men's Clothing

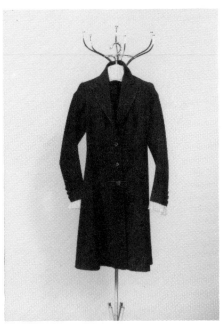

Men's vintage apparel is highly collectible, but much harder to find. Presently, most popular for collecting are rayon Hawaiian shirts from the 1940s and 1950s. Pleated pants from that period are also sought avidly. Tuxedos with tails, which are very much in demand, are bringing high prices, as are silk or beaver top hats. These are particularly popular with antique car buffs and patrons of the theater.

Dress coat, black gabardine, white lace cuffs, silk lining, c. 1870-1880, **$60-70.**

Dress coat, gray and black pin stripe wool, silk lined, c. 1880-1890, **$55-65.**

Dress coat, black wool, silk lined, poodle collar and cuffs, c. 1890-1910, **$60-75.**

Dress coat, purple velvet, silk lined, c. 1890-1905, **$40-50.**

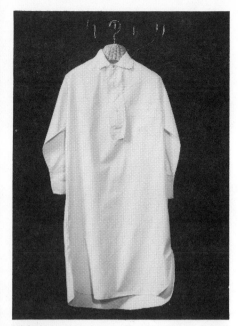

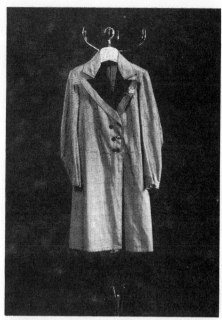

Nightshirt, white cotton with eyelet trim, c. 1890-1905, **$80-90.**

Dress coat, black wool, silk collar and lining, c. 1895-1900, **$65-80.**

Dress coat, navy and white plaid wool, c. 1900-1910, **$45-55.**

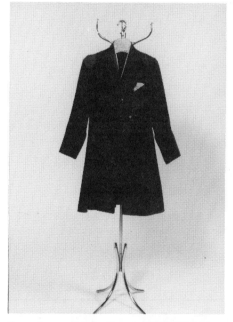

Dress coat, black gabardine, silk lined, c. 1900-1910, **$50-60.**

Brown dress coat, heavy linen, c. 1900-1910, **$45-55.**

Brown velvet smoking jacket, silk quilted collar, cuffs, pockets, silk lined, c. 1900-1910, **$70-80.**

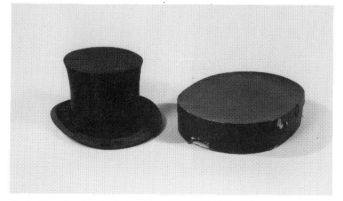

Black silk, collapsible top hat, original box, 1900-1910, **$80-100.**

Spats, gray wool, c. 1900-1910, **$20-25.**

Spats, blue wool, c. 1900-1910, **$18-22.**

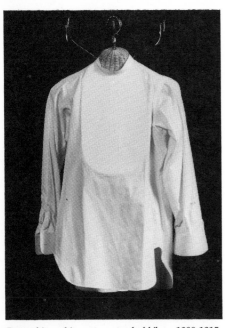

Dress shirt, white cotton, starched bib, c. 1900-1915, **$30-35.**

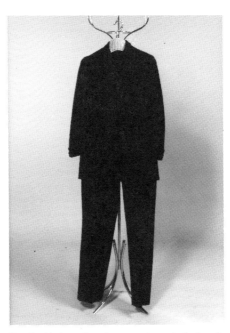

Tuxedo, black wool, cutaway coat, pants button in front, c. 1900-1910, **$100-125.**

Suit, casual, black and white checked, pearl buttons, c. 1900-1910, **$80-100.**

White tuxedo vest, c. 1900-1915, **$25-30.**

Black wool vest, c. 1900-1915, **$25-30.**

Right: *Ball gown, pink, lined with blue and pink plaid silk crepe de chine, yellow chiffon high collar and sleeves. Self purse attaches at side with enameled buckle. Has matching silk petticoat with ecru lace dust ruffle, c. 1875-1890,* **$275-300.**

Below left: *Silk velvet bodice, trimmed with self-colored piping embroidery and oriental style brocade, c. 1880-1895,* **$95-125.**

Below right: *Dress hat, pleated pink silk and fuchsia velvet, c. 1880-1895,* **$70-80.**

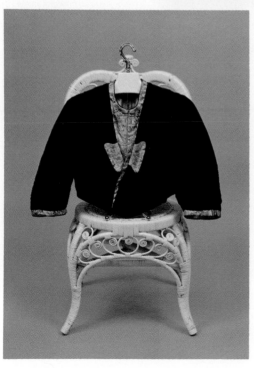

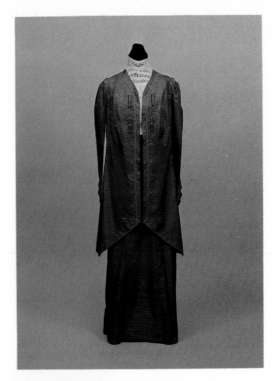

Above left: *Ball gown, yellow silk crepe de chine and ruby silk velvet with built-in corset, c. 1885-1900,* **$300-350.**

Above right: *Walking suit, wine-colored silk with self-colored piping embroidery, ivory silk high-neck waist with cutwork yoke and silk fringe, c. 1885-1900,* **$275-300.**

Left: *Day dress, magenta and white floral print silk with black lace trim, white lace high collar, lego-o-mutton sleeves, c. 1885-1895,* **$225-250.**

Above left: *Purse, dark brown velvet with brass frame embellished with paste amethyst jewels, c. 1890-1900,* **$80-100.**

Above right: *Evening dress, royal blue gabardine, net and silk satin, self-colored piping embroidery, white lace and black velvet trim, c. 1890-1905,* **$200-225.**

Right: *Tea dress, pink linen with self-colored lace trim, white lace high collar, c. 1890-1905,* **$275-300.**

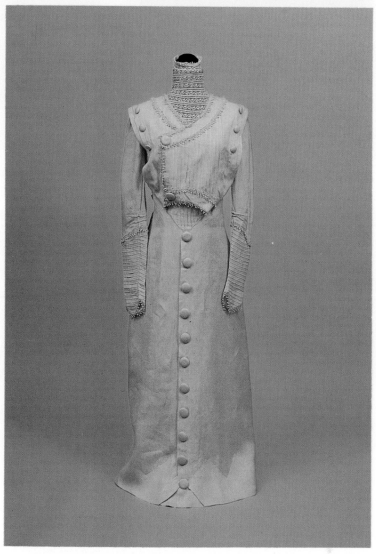

Above: *Fan, peacock feathers, hand-carved wooden sticks, c. 1910-1920,* **$75-90.**

Left: *Blouse, pink and mint green silk georgette, hand-painted floral design, c. 1920-1930,* **$90-100.**

Right: *Opera cape, black gabardine with hand-embroidery, silk lined, c. 1920-1930,* **$250-300.**

Below left: *Beaded dress, blue silk velvet, hand-beaded with white glass beads, c. 1920-1930,* **$300-325.**

Below right: *Beaded purse, hand beaded in a colorful paisley design, silk lining, celluloid frame, c. 1920-1930,* **$80-90.**

Above left: *Shawl, colorful Art Deco style, floral print silk with hand-tied silk fringe, measures six feet square, including fringe,* **$150-175.**

Above right: *Jean Patou cape, pink silk with ostrich feathers, label reads "Jean Patou, 7 Rue St. Florentin, Paris 92888," c. 1920-1932,* **$275-300.**

Left: *Gold sequined evening dress made for movie star Ann Sothern, label reads "Ann Sothern 4155,"* **$450-500.**

Above left: *Dress, blue silk chiffon with bubble print, ecru lace inset, c. 1925-1935,* **$70-90.**

Above right: *Evening dress, white and yellow silk crepe de chine, gold lamé; white lace tunic is hand beaded with white bugle beads. Two Chinese hand-embroidered silk panels are attached at the low waistline, c. 1920-1930,* **$500-550.**

Right: *Silk evening dress, colorful floral print, cut on the bias, low backline, c. 1930-1940,* **$80-100.**

Left: *Rayon nightgown, colorful floral print, cut on the bias, c. 1930-1940,* **$35-45.**

Below left: *Suit, ecru woven rayon, white built-in dickey, high padded shoulders, two-tiered self-peplum, celluloid buttons, c. 1935-1940,* **$90-100.**

Below right: *Evening dress, colorful paisley print rayon, label reads "Steinbergs, Tenth and Olive, St. Louis, Missouri," c. 1935-1940,* **$90-110.**

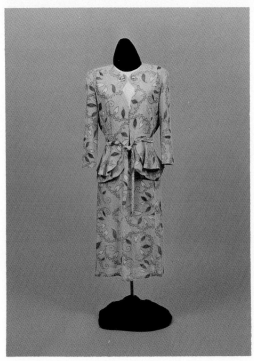

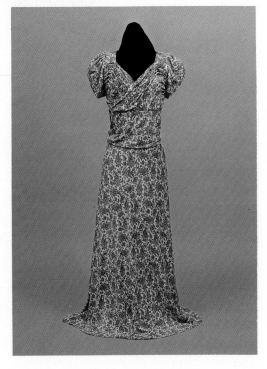

Extra Long Suspenders.

No. 34R729 Men's Extra Length Plain White or Slate Color Elastic Web Suspenders, made same style as No. 34R728, 40 inches long. Fine and first class in every particular. Price, per pair........45c
If by mail, postage extra, per pair, 5 cents.

Men's Lisle Suspenders, 35 Cents.

No. 34R731 Men's Fancy Suspenders, made from fine quality lisle elastic webbing, 1⅛ inches wide, the same quality that is used in almost all suspenders sold for 50 cents a pair. A smooth surface, light weight suspender, comfortable for summer wear. Fancy design similar to illustration. Fine gilt buckles, kid ends and snap button cast-off. Our low price is made possible by purchasing these goods in quantities from maker for cash. This quality will please and you can save 15 cents. Medium colors.
Per pair......$0.35
Per dozen.... 4.20
If by mail, postage extra, 5c.

Extra Fine Silk Embroidered Suspenders.

No. 34R732 Men's Extra Fine Silk Embroidered Suspenders. Handsome ornamental gold slides and castoff. Braided lisle ends and drawer supporters. New exclusive patterns. Light, medium and dark colors. Artistic and elaborate silk embroidery. Charming and effective contrasts. Per pair. 40c
If by mail, postage extra, per pair, 5 cents.

The Guyot.

No. 34R740 Bretelle's Universelles. The Famous French Sanitary Suspenders. Light weight, strong, linen web, with elastic in back pieces only. Unexcelled for comfort and durability. Light and dark colors. All colors absolutely fast. Per pair..42c
If by mail, postage extra, per pair, 5 cents.

The Parisian Suspender.

No. 34R744 The New Parisian Suspender. Made of finest imported elastic web in plaids and stripes of medium colors. Full length, cross back, kid trimmed with duplicate rolled and stitched leather ends, one running on the metal, the other on the leather. Thus the strain is equalized, making an unusually attractive and dependable suspender. Regular retail value, 75 cents.
Price, pair....42c
If by mail, postage extra, per pair, 5 cents.

The President Suspender.

No. 34R746 A new style recently patented suspender with improved back which equalizes the strain on all parts with every attitude. Relieves the strain on shoulders and not likely to pull off buttons. Made with strong non-elastic web cord in back and high grade elastic webbing in main parts. Every pair warranted to wear to the entire satisfaction of the purchaser. Made in fancy webs or plain colors.
Price, per pair........$0.45
Per dozen... 5.40

If by mail, postage extra, per pair, 5c.

Men's suspenders, Sears, Roebuck & Co. Catalogue, c. 1902, **$15-20 each.**

STYLE 16
Chesterfield or Straight Front Frock

Back View   Front View
STYLE 5
One Button Cutaway Frock

Chesterfield and cutaway suits from Sears and Roebuck, c. 1902, **$100-150 each.**

FANCY BOSOM DRESS SHIRTS.

No. 16R143 Men's Fine Dress Shirts; made with medium length bosoms, with pair of link cuffs; Garner's fine percale; gusset facings with patent splice at back buttonhole to prevent collar button from rubbing the neck. We have these goods in blue and white, pink and white, red and white and black and white stripes. Give color you prefer and you will be pleased with our selection. Open front and back. Sizes, 14, 14½, 15, 15½, 16, 16½, 17, 17½ and 18. What size do you wear?
Price for three, $2.70; each..90c

Men's All Colored Dress Shirts, 85c.

No. 16R150 Men's Fine Dress Shirts; made medium length bosom, with one pair of link cuffs to match. A strictly high grade shirt; made from Garner's fine percale, which is the standard of the world in quality. Gussets, facings, with patent splice at back buttonhole to prevent collar button from rubbing the neck. We have the most select designs offered this season in blues, pinks, red and green stripes, in combinations, such as blue and white, pink and white, etc. Give color preference and you will be pleased with our selection. The usual retail value of such shirts is $1.25. Open front and back. Sizes, 14, 14½, 15, 15½, 16, 16½, 17, 17½, 18. What size do you wear?
Price, six for $5.10; three for $2.55; each...................85c
If by mail, postage extra, each, 13 cents.

Men's Fine Madras Shirt, $1.30.

No. 16R152 Men's Fine Madras Shirts, made with medium length bosom, the comfortable kind. A strictly high grade shirt in every respect that will meet the demands of exacting dressers. We guarantee every shirt perfect fitting. There is no improvement known to the shirtmaker's art that is not to be found in this shirt. We cannot recommend a shirt of this kind too highly for wear, appearance, comfort and fast color. The colors are mainly in blue, pink and oxblood backgrounds overshot in contrasting colors in a large variety of stripes and figured effects. Shirts of this quality are invariably cheap in the end, and as all our patterns in these goods are up to date and new you will make no mistake in ordering this number. State color preference. Made open front and back, with pocket buttonhole at back of neck. One pair of fashionable link cuffs. Sizes, 14, 14½, 15, 15½, 16, 16½ and 17.
Price, each.............................$1.30
If by mail, postage extra, 13 cents.

Men's Colored Shirts with Detachable Collars and Cuffs.

No. 16R160 Men's Fine French Percale Shirts, with detachable collars and cuffs; fast colors; open back; medium length bosom. They are made large and full sized body, and we guarantee them to give perfect satisfaction. Two detachable lay down collars and one pair of cuffs are included with each shirt. These goods do not retail for less than $1.00 each. Neat stripes and checks, such as blue, brown and pink on white background; also in scroll or all over effects. Sizes, 14½, 15, 15½, 16, 16½, 17.
Price, six for $4.80; three for $2.40; each................80c
If by mail, postage extra, each, 15 cents.

Men's dress shirts advertised in the 1902 Sears, Roebuck & Co. Catalogue, **$30-35 each.**

MEN'S PATENT LEATHER BUTTON, $2.25.

IMPORTED CLOTH TOP.

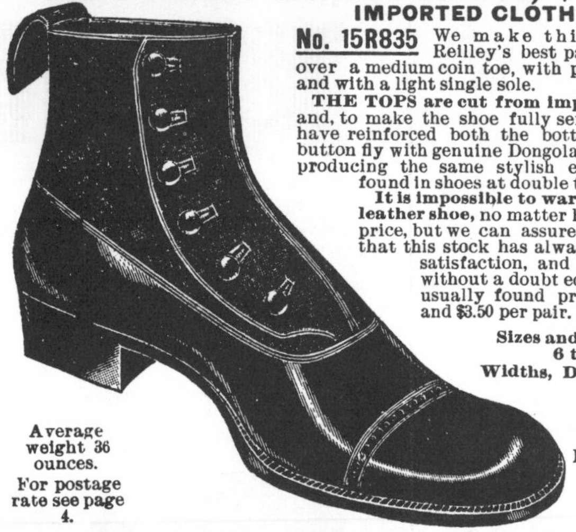

No. 15R835 We make this shoe from Reilley's best patent leather over a medium coin toe, with perforated tip and with a light single sole.

THE TOPS are cut from imported serge, and, to make the shoe fully serviceable, we have reinforced both the bottoms and the button fly with genuine Dongola kid, thereby producing the same stylish effect usually found in shoes at double this price.

It is impossible to warrant a patent leather shoe, no matter how high the price, but we can assure our patrons that this stock has always given fair satisfaction, and this shoe is without a doubt equal to those usually found priced at $3.00 and $3.50 per pair.

Sizes and half sizes, 6 to 11.
Widths, D, E and EE.

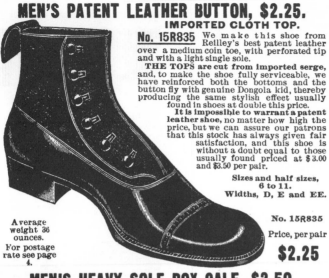

Average weight 36 ounces.
For postage rate see page 4.

No. 15R835
Price, per pair
$2.25

MEN'S HEAVY SOLE BOX CALF, $2.50.

GOODYEAR WELT. A $4.00 SHOE FOR $2.50.

No. 15R837 THE LATEST FAD among shoe dealers is to name a shoe and advertise it as their special $4.00 shoe. We made arrangements with one of the largest manufacturers of strictly high grade shoes, a maker you would all recognize if we were allowed to tell his name, to run his special line of $4.00 shoes and to sell them at our own prices, providing, of course, the name was not mentioned.

This shoe is sold by some of the largest stores in the country at $4.00 and even at that price is excellent value. It is made from White Bros.' box calf leather over the very latest English last, with fancy perforated tip. The soles are cut from genuine California oak sole leather, made extra heavy and with full extended edges, thereby protecting the uppers and insuring a thoroughly durable shoe. This shoe is genuine Goodyear welt sewn, fitted with bleached calf inside stay and a custom outside back stay. **We want your order** for a pair of these shoes, for we feel that the best advertising we can possibly get is to demonstrate to our patrons the fact that we can and do furnish this strictly high grade $4.00 shoe for little more than half its actual worth.

Sizes and half sizes, 5 to 12.
Widths, A, B, C, D, E and EE.

Average weight, 83 ounces.
For postage rate see page 4.
No. 15R837 Price, per pair..**$2.50**

A MODERN PATENT LEATHER OXFORD FOR MEN.

No. 15R846 **A shoe worthy of your consideration. A delightfully easy, stylish and perfect fitting shoe, a standard of real shoe excellence.** To produce a genuine Goodyear welt Oxford of such quality as the one we herewith illustrate has never been attempted before by any manufacturer at the price we quote. The stock is excellent quality of patent leather vamp and heel foxing, cut in the very newest style, handsomely perforated and stitched. The top is of genuine pebble calf and the contrast produces an effect seldom found in a man's Oxford at any price. **The inner sole, outer sole, trimmings, etc., are all of select material and highly finished throughout. This is a shoe fitted for swell dressers.** Oxfords were never more in demand than at the present time, we are the leaders in Oxfords and this Oxford is our leader. Owing to the great effort on our part to build this shoe and on account of such a small margin of profit we are able to offer our customers one of the best shoes for the money that has ever been sold by any house in the country.

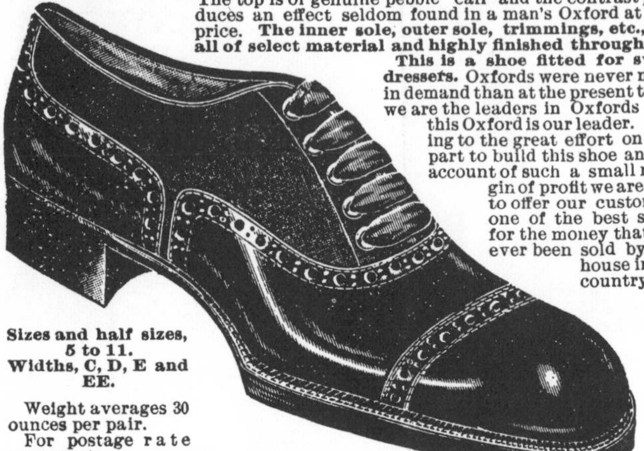

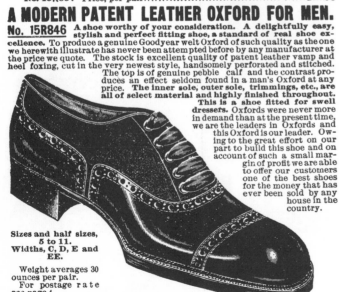

Sizes and half sizes, 5 to 11.
Widths, C, D, E and EE.

Weight averages 30 ounces per pair.
For postage rate see page 4.

No. 15R846 Price, per pair..**$2.55**

Men's shoes advertised in the 1902 Sears, Roebuck & Co. Catalogue. *Button shoes,* **$50-60;** *lace shoes,* **$30-35.**

A REMINDER. **Do not forget to give size for collars or cuffs. Your order will then have prompt attention.**

IF BY MAIL, postage on collars extra, per dozen, 15 cents; each, 2 cents. Cuffs, postage extra, per dozen, 20 cents; per pair, 2 cents.

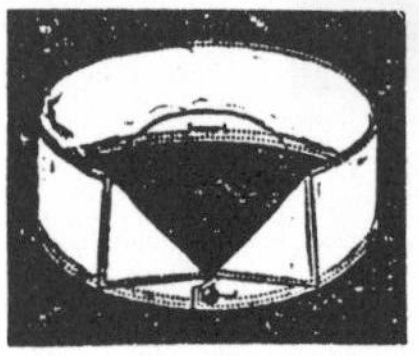

No. 34R20
Front, 1⅞-in. Back, 1⅝-in.

No. 34R20 Men's Linen Collars. Sizes, 14 to 18.
Each.............**$0.10**
Per dozen........ **1.20**

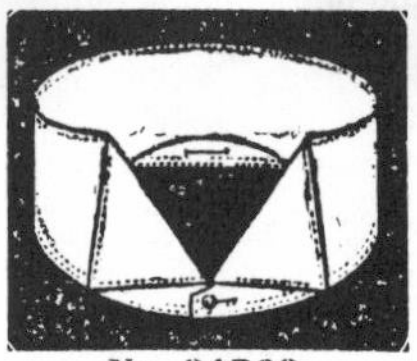

No. 34R23
Front, 2¼-in. Back, 2-in.

No. 34R23 Men's Linen Collars. Sizes, 14 to 17.
Each.............**$0.10**
Per dozen........ **1.20**

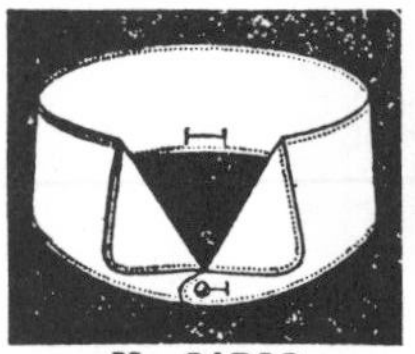

No. 34R28
Front, 2½-in. Back, 2⅜-in.

No. 34R28 Men's Linen Collars. Sizes, 14 to 17.
Each.............**$0.10**
Per dozen........ **1.20**

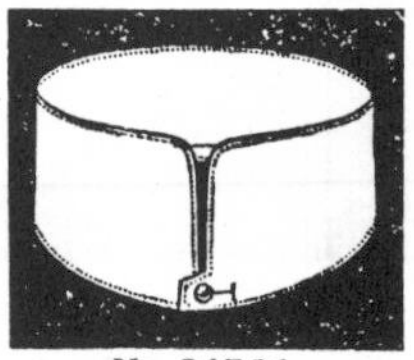

No. 34R31
Front, 2⅛-in. Back, 1⅝-in.

No. 34R31 Men's Linen Collars. Sizes, 14 to 17.
Each.............**$0.10**
Per dozen........ **1.20**

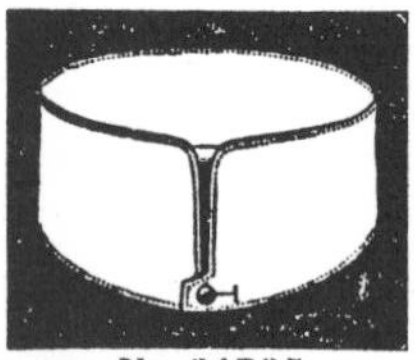

No. 34R35
Front, 2⅝-in. Back, 2¼-in.

No. 34R35 Men's Linen Collars. Sizes, 14 to 17.
Each.............**$0.10**
Per dozen........ **1.20**

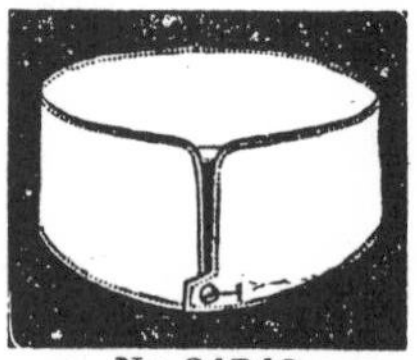

No. 34R40
Front, 3-in. Back, 2½-in.

No. 34R40 Men's Linen Collars. Sizes, 14 to 16½.
Each.............**$0.10**
Per dozen........ **1.20**

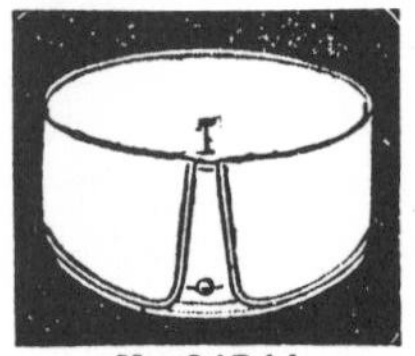

No. 34R44
Front, 3-in. Back, 2¾-in.

No. 34R44 Men's Linen Collars. Sizes, 14 to 16½.
Each.............**$0.10**
Per dozen........ **1.20**

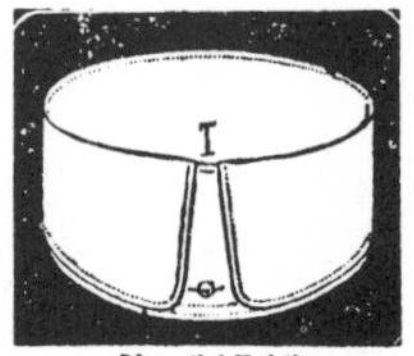

No. 34R46
Front, 2½-in. Back, 2¼-in.

No. 34R46 Men's Linen Collars. Sizes, 14 to 16½. Each......**$0.10**
Per dozen........ **1.20**

Men's linen collars advertised in the 1902 Sears, Roebuck & Co. Catalogue, **$5-10 each.**

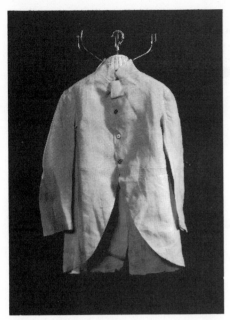

Dress coat, cutaway style, ecru linen, c. 1910-1915, **$40-50.**

Golfing knickers, brown wool, never worn, c. 1910-1920, **$30-35.**

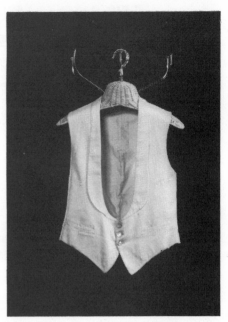

White tuxedo vest, c. 1910-1925, **$20-30.**

Black cotton cummerbund, adjustable, c. 1910-1920, **$15-18.**

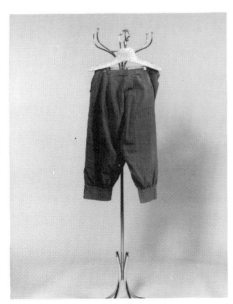

Hunting knickers, khaki cotton, side button, c. 1910-1920, **$20-30.**

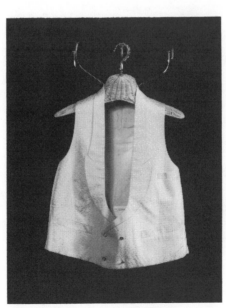

White tuxedo vest, c. 1910-1925, **$20-25.**

Vest, brown and beige check, never worn, c. 1910-1920, **$20-25.**

139

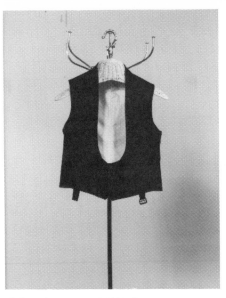

Vest, gray and black striped satin, c. 1910-1920, **$25-30.**

Black wool vest, c. 1910-1920, **$20-25.**

Ivy League golf cap, wool, c. 1920-1930, **$15-18.**

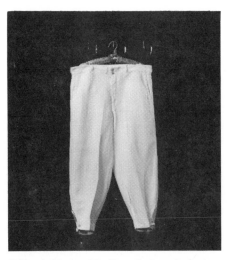

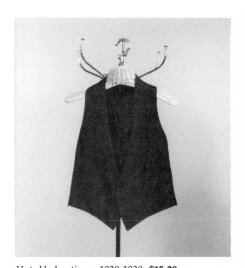

Top hat, felt with silk ribbon, c. 1920-1930, **$45-55.**

Golfing knickers, white linen, buttons in front, c. 1920-1930, **$40-50.**

Vest, black satin, c. 1920-1930, **$15-20.**

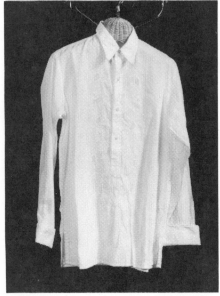

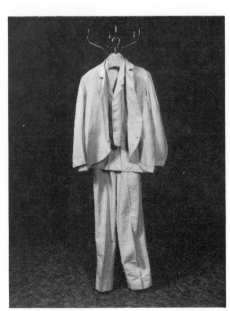

Dress shirt, white cotton, hand-embroidery, pearl buttons, c. 1920-1930, **$30-40.**

Palm Beach suit, three-piece linen, pearl buttons, c. 1915-1920, **$70-100.**

Black wool tuxedo with tails, silk lapels, c. 1920-1930, **$140-160.**

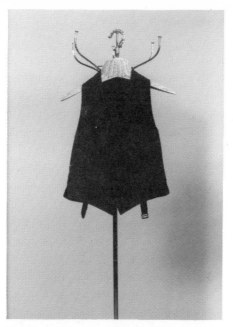

Vest, black wool, c. 1920-1930, **$18-25.**

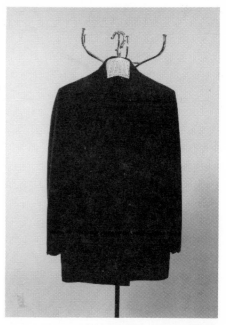

Navy wool blazer, double-breasted, c. 1925-1940, **$25-35.**

Salvation Army hat with rain cover, c. 1925-1935, **$35-45.**

Dinner jacket, white linen, Palm Beach label, c. 1930-1935, **$25-35.**

Smoking jacket, royal blue silk brocade, quilted silk shawl collar, c. 1930-1940, **$80-90.**

141

Fedora, black felt, satin ribbon, original box, c. 1935-1940, **$30-45.**

Reversible robe, navy striped satin, fringed belt, c. 1935-1940, **$45-55.**

Blazer, yellow and blue pinstripe, double-breasted, c. 1940-1945, **$20-30.**

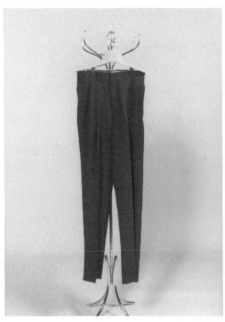

Pleated pants, brown gabardine, never worn, c. 1940-1950, **$20-25.**

Cummberbund, black and plaid satin, c. 1940-1950, **$10-15.**

Robe, red dotted rayon satin, padded shoulders, c. 1940-1950, **$40-50.**

Navy uniform shirt, blue wool, c. 1940-1950, **$10-15.**

Western style blazer, brown gabardine, c. 1950-1955, **$30-35.**

Dinner jacket, white, satin lined, c. 1950-1960, **$30-40.**

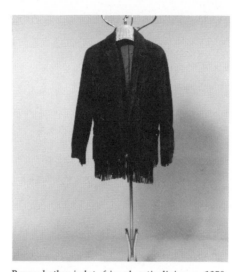

Brown leather jacket, fringed, satin lining, c. 1950-1960, **$40-50.**

Pajamas, red and white tropical print acetate, c. 1950-1960, **$35-40.**

Rayon shirt, casual, tropical print, label reads "Made in Hawaii," c. 1950-1960, **$40-50.**

Rayon shirt, casual, multicolored paisley print, label reads "Made in California," c. 1950-1960, **$35-40.**

Cotton shirt, casual, tropical print, c. 1950-1960, **$30-35.**

143

Cotton shirt, casual, multicolored print, c. 1950-1960, **$30-35.**

Shirt, casual, black and gray striped acetate, c. 1950-1955, **$20-25.**

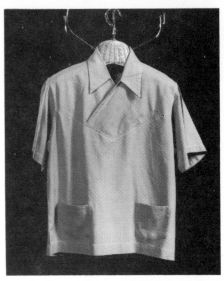

Casual pullover, chambray, c. 1950-1960, **$12-15.**

Shirt, casual, gray, black, and yellow wool plaid, c. 1950-1960, **$15-20.**

Sports shirt, gray flannel, c. 1950-1955, **$20-25.**

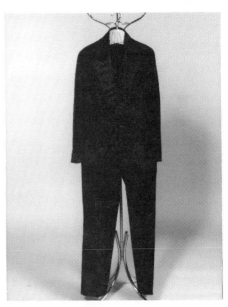

Tuxedo, black wool, satin lapels, c. 1950-1960, **$40-60.**

Red wool vest, c. 1950-1960, **$10-15.**

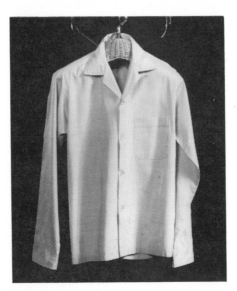

Shirt, casual, green polished cotton, hand-tailored, c. 1955-1965, **$10-15.**

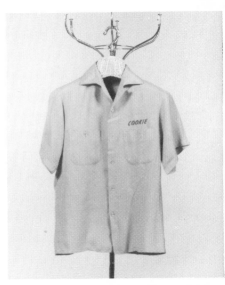

Bowling shirt, green rayon, c. 1955-1960, **$15-20.**

Shirt, casual, plaid linen, shades of rust, c. 1955-1960, **$15-20.**

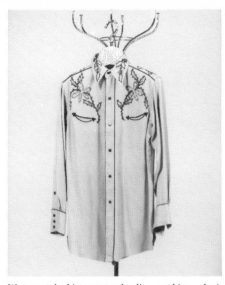

Western style shirt, green gabardine, machine embroidery, c. 1955-1960, **$45-60.**

Shirt, western style, black cotton, c. 1960-1965, **$15-20.**

Shirt, casual, burgundy print on white cotton, c. 1960-1965, **$10-15.**

Tuxedo, gold and black brocade, wool pants, c. 1960-1965, **$40-50.**

Hawaiian shirt, casual, ecru and brown rayon-cotton blend c. 1960, **$20-25.**

Robe, black rayon brocade with oriental machine embroidery, c. 1970, **$30-35.**

Children's Clothing

Children's vintage apparel is fun to collect. The styles of the past are charming and one can spend hours admiring early pieces. Christening gowns are most popular, with many people buying them for their own infants. Antique doll collectors seek some of the early apparel for their dolls. The earliest pieces, and especially those which were handmade or lavishly trimmed with laces or hand embroidery, bring the highest prices.

Infant sweater set, red, hand-knit, c. 1870-1880, **$40-45.**

Suits for boys ages 8 to 10 on the left and ages 5 to 7 on the right, from Victorian Fashions and Costumes, **$75-90 each.**

Christening dress, handmade, white cotton with tucks and hand-embroidered eyelet trim, c. 1880-1900, **$75-90.**

*Child's dress, ecru lace and net, silk lining, c. 1880-1890, **$120-140.***

*Boy's dress, white cotton with hand-embroidery, c. 1880-1900, **$45-60.***

*White flannel slip, hand-embroidered with crocheted lace, c. 1880-1900, **$20-30.***

Confirmation dresses, c. 1881, from Victorian Fashions and Costumes, **$175-200 each.**

*Toddler slip, white cotton, handmade with eyelet and tucks, c. 1890-1900, **$40-45.***

*White flannel slip, handmade, c. 1890-1900, **$15-20.***

Infants' and small children's wear, c. 1893, from Victorian Fashions and Costumes. *Left: pique coat,* **$60-80.** *Center: frock,* **$55-75.** *Right: cashmere wrapper,* **$80-100.**

Small boys' costumes from Victorian Fashions and Costumes. *Left: boy's white duck suit,* **$40-60.** *Top center: boy's suit with kilt and reefer jacket,* **$100-125.** *Bottom center: boy's white pique frock,* **$90-110.** *Right: boy's one-piece pleated frock,* **$35-55.**

149

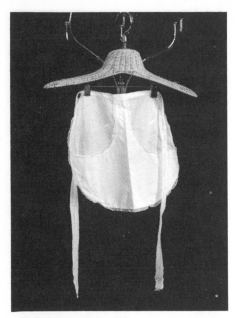

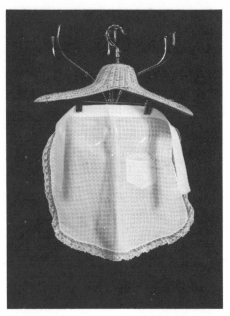

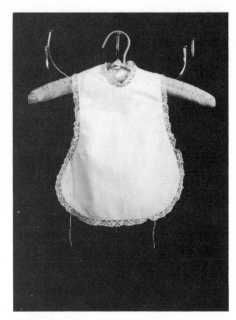

Toddler's apron, white cotton, c. 1900-1910, **$8-10.**

Child's apron, white cotton with lace trim, c. 1900-1910, **$5-10.**

White cotton bib, c. 1900-1910, **$5-7.**

Baby cap, white, hand-crocheted, c. 1900-1910, **$30-35.**

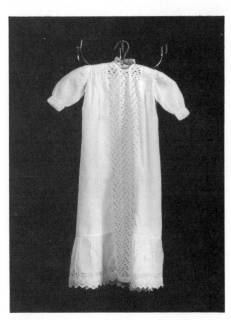

Christening dress, white cotton, handmade with eyelet insets, c. 1900-1910, **$40-50.**

Christening gown with matching slip, white cotton eyelet, 42 inches long, c. 1900-1910, **$90-120.**

Boy's christening dress, handmade, white cotton with eyelet inset and trim, c. 1900-1910, **$55-65.**

White corduroy cloak, handmade, c. 1900-1910, **$30-40.**

Communion dress, white cotton with eyelet and lace trim, c. 1900-1920, **$70-90.**

Communion dress, handmade, white cotton with hand-embroidery, handmade lace, tucks, c. 1900-1920, **$90-100.**

Slip, white cotton with eyelet trim and pearl buttons, c. 1900-1910, **$25-30.**

Shoes, two-tone, leather, lace-up, c. 1900-1910, **$20-30.**

White cotton skirt, with tucks and eyelet, c. 1900-1910, **$30-40.**

Infants' cloaks from Sears and Roebuck, c. 1902, **$70-85 each.**

No. 38R1641
Child's Cap, suitable for little boy or girl, made of white cotton pique, with heavy blue polka dot band and shield. A very popular spring and summer cap.

Price.....................25c
If by mail, postage extra, 4c

No. 38R1642 **Child's Cap,** made of good quality pressed flannel, white fancy band around peak of cap, and fancy design on top of crown of soutache braid; the cap is lined and well made. Colors, cardinal or navy blue. Price........24c
If by mail, postage extra, 10 cents.

No. 38R1643 This is a very neat little cap, made of all wool flannel, fancy ornamental design on crown of silk braid, as shown in illustration. Black velvet rim and peak, black velvet covered button on top of crown, satin lined. A very neat and dressy little cap. Colors, cardinal or navy blue. Price, 41c
If by mail, postage extra, 12c

No. 38R1644 This is a very stylish and dressy little cap for boys. Made of good quality velvette; the rim is made of a fancy mixture of cloth, with a double row of silk cord around front; satin lined. Colors, black only.
Price...................49c
If by mail, postage extra, 12 cents.

No. 38R1645
Child's Toque. Turkish design. Made of nice quality flannel; very ornamental in design; around the crown are two bands of fancy braid, and over the flowing end of the crown seven rows of band trimming as shown in illustration. Silk tassel on end of cap; cap is lined, and a very excellent value. Colors, cardinal or navy.
Price, each **(If by mail, postage extra, 8 cents) 23c**

No. 38R1646 **Child's Toque.** Oriental design, combination design, made of good quality black velvette and all wool cardinal flannel; with two rows of gold silk soutache braid around brim, while the crown has braided rows of gold soutache braid with gold spikes on ends. (See illustration.) Long silk tassel on end; this is a very original and pretty design.
Price, each........48c
If by mail, postage extra, 8 cents.

Boys' and children's caps and toques available from Sears and Roebuck, c. 1902, **$10-35 each.**

Children's dresses from Sears and Roebuck, c. 1902, **$30-45 each.**

Walking cloaks for children ages 1 to 5, advertised in the 1902 Sears, Roebuck & Co. Catalogue, $50-75 each.

Girls' white lawn dresses advertised in the 1902 Sears, Roebuck & Co. Catalogue, $70-100 each.

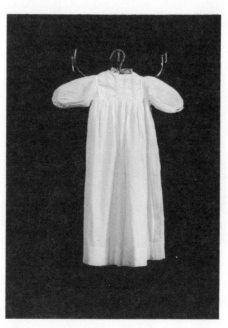

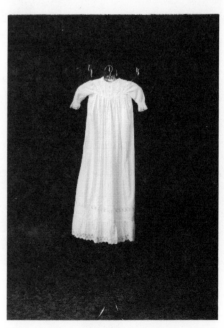

Christening dress, white cotton with eyelet trim, 38 inches long, c. 1905, $65-70.

Christening dress, white cotton with eyelet yoke, c. 1910-1920, $35-40.

Christening dress, white cotton with tucks and eyelet trim, 38 inches long, c. 1910-1920, $75-85.

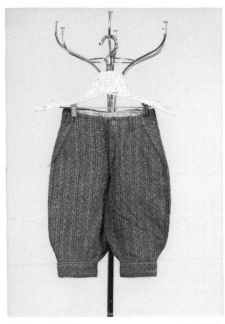

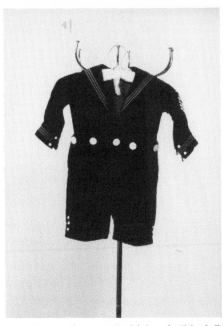

Boy's wool knickers, never worn, c. 1910-1920, **$20-30.**

Shoes, black leather, lace-up, c. 1910-1920, **$12-18.**

Boy's brown velveteen suit, label reads "Marshall, Field and Company," c. 1910-1920, **$75-90.**

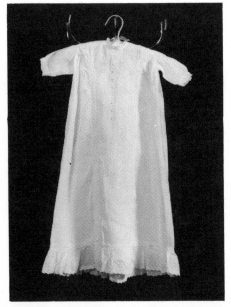

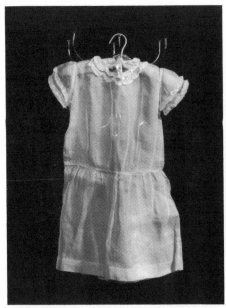

Christening dress, white cotton with fine eyelet inset and trim, c. 1920-1930, **$40-45.**

Black leather shoes, c. 1920-1930, **$15-20.**

Child's dress, yellow, c. 1920-1930, **$15-20.**

Wind shawl, hand-knit, c. 1920-1930, **$20-22.**

Glossary

Agrafe. A decorative metal clasp or hook and eye covered with braid.

Basque. A jacket-like bodice, fitting close to the body and usually ending below the waist in a short peplum or skirt.

Broderie Anglaise. A lace in which holes are punched out of a fabric and then oversewn for firmness to form a lacy design.

Casaque. A light coat-like garment worn outdoors.

Chemise. A garment similar to a loose, short slip.

Chemisette. A vestee or dickey, generally sleeveless, used primarily to fill low necklines.

Cravat bow. A bow worn at the neck.

Fichu. A small shawl or scarf worn over the shoulders and tied in front.

Grosgrain. A fabric or ribbon with heavy ribs woven horizontally.

Jet. A hard, black variety of lignite used in making jewelry and beads.

Mantle. A loose cloak.

Paletot. A loose cloak with one or more cape collars.

Passementerie. Trims such as braid, cords, or heavy embroidery.

Pelerine. A short shoulder cape.

Peplum. A short extension of a bodice or jacket flaring out below the waist.

Petticoat. Another term for underskirt.

Polonaise. A coat-gown with the front of the skirt pulled back over an underskirt.

Point lace. A term for needlepoint lace made entirely of buttonhole stitches.

Sacque. An unfitted or semi-fitted bodice, jacket, or robe.

Toilette. A dress or outfit.

Tulle. Silk net.

Ulster. A long, loose fitting overcoat worn by men or women.

Waist. Another term for blouse.

Yoke. A fitted or shaped piece at the top of a skirt or at the shoulder of a garment.

Bibliography

Battersby, Martin. *Decorative Thirties*. New York, N.Y.: Walker and Co., 1971.

Blum, Stella, editor. *Victorian Fashions and Costumes from Harper's Bazar, 1867-1898*. New York, N.Y.: Dover Publications, Inc., 1974.

Funaro, Diana. *The Yestermorrow Clothes Book*. Radnor, Pa.: Chilton Book Company, 1976.

Howell, Georgina. *In Vogue*. New York, N.Y.: Penguin Books, Inc., 1979.

Lynam, Ruth, editor. *Couture, An Illustrated History of the Great Paris Designers and Their Creations*. Garden City, N.Y.: Doubleday and Company, 1972.

Milinaire, Caterine, and Troy, Carol. *Cheap Chic*. New York, N.Y.: Crown Publishers, Inc., 1978.

Schiff, Stefan O. *Buttons, Art in Miniature*. Berkeley, Calif.: Lancaster-Miller Publishers, 1979.

Index

About the Author

Photograph courtesy *Pueblo Star Journal and Chieftain* c. 1979

Sheila Malouff is the owner of Essentially Chic Wholesale Vintage Clothing. At one time the owner and operator of a retail vintage clothing store, Ms. Malouff has been a collector of vintage clothing and accessories for twelve years.

She has traveled across the United States buying and selling vintage clothing. Her business brings her in contact with retailers and other wholesalers of vintage clothing in every section of the continental United States, as well as Alaska and Hawaii. Because she has sold vintage clothing to more than one hundred retail stores in virtually every state in the nation, Ms. Malouff is uniquely qualified in pricing vintage clothing and accessories. Her own extensive collection and inventory make up the bulk of the listings in this book.

In addition to writing this price guide and running her own successful wholesale business, Ms. Malouff has traveled extensively in the last six years appraising larger vintage clothing collections for various estates. A member of the Antique Appraisal Association of America, Inc., she has also conducted many fashion shows for charities, using apparel from her personal collection.

Ms. Malouff resides in Pueblo, Colorado, with her husband, Charles, and their two children.